Practising Gender Equality in Education

Oxfam GB

Oxfam GB, founded in 1942, is a development, humanitarian, and campaigning agency dedicated to finding lasting solutions to poverty and suffering around the world. Oxfam believes that every human being is entitled to a life of dignity and opportunity, and it works with others worldwide to make this become a reality.

From its base in Oxford in the United Kingdom, Oxfam GB publishes and distributes a wide range of books and other resource materials for development and relief workers, researchers and campaigners, schools and colleges, and the general public, as part of its programme of advocacy, education, and communications.

Oxfam GB is a member of Oxfam International, a confederation of 13 agencies of diverse cultures and languages, which share a commitment to working for an end to injustice and poverty – both in long-term development work and at times of crisis.

For further information about Oxfam's publishing, and online ordering, visit **www.oxfam.org.uk/publications**

For information about Oxfam's development, advocacy, and humanitarian relief work around the world, visit **www.oxfam.org.uk**

Beyond Access Project

The chapters in this book were originally produced as papers by the Beyond Access Project. They form a series of papers written to inform public debate on development and humanitarian policy issues. For further information about the Beyond Access Project, see:
www.ioe.ac.uk/efps/beyondaccess

For comments on issues raised in this book, please email:
beyondaccess@oxfam.org.uk

The papers in this book can be found online in French, Spanish, and Portuguese at: http://publications.oxfam.org.uk/oxfam/results.asp?ISBN=9780855985974

Practising Gender Equality in Education

Edited by Sheila Aikman and Elaine Unterhalter

Oxfam

First published by Oxfam GB in 2007

© Oxfam GB 2007

Chapters 1–9 first appeared online as a series of papers in December 2005 © Oxfam GB 2005.
The introduction, conclusion, and all other matter is original to this edition © Oxfam GB 2007.
Chapters 1–9 have been edited slightly from their original formats (online pdf files) for this book.
The versions contained in this book are the definitive ones for future citation.

ISBN 978 0 85598 598 1

A catalogue record for this publication is available from the British Library.

Available from:
Bournemouth English Book Centre, PO Box 1496, Parkstone, Dorset, BH12 3YD, UK
tel: +44 (0)1202 712933; fax: +44 (0)1202 712930; email: oxfam@bebc.co.uk

USA: Stylus Publishing LLC, PO Box 605, Herndon, VA 20172-0605, USA
tel: +1 (0)703 661 1581; fax: +1 (0)703 661 1547; email: styluspub@aol.com

For details of local agents and representatives in other countries, consult our website:
www.oxfam.org.uk/publications
or contact Oxfam Publishing, Oxfam House, John Smith Drive, Cowley, Oxford OX4 2JY, UK
tel: +44 (0)1865 311 311; fax: +44 (0)1865 312 600; email: publish@oxfam.org.uk

Our website contains a fully searchable database of all our titles, and facilities for secure
on-line ordering.

Cover image: Boy and girl aged 5, going to school. (Andaman Islands).
(Rajendra Shaw/Oxfam)

Published by Oxfam GB, Oxfam House, John Smith Drive, Cowley, Oxford OX4 2JY, UK.

Printed by Information Press, Eynsham.

Oxfam GB is a registered charity, no. 202 918, and is a member of Oxfam International.

Contents

Acknowledgements

This book is an outcome of the Beyond Access: Gender, Education and Development project. Many people have contributed to the work of the project since 2003 and particularly to the thinking that is distilled in these chapters. Chapters 1–3 draw on ideas generated in the six Beyond Access seminars that took place between May 2003 and February 2005. In writing up themes from the seminars we want to acknowledge the contribution made by all those who participated during the events and in ongoing discussions. Chapter 4 has been developed from discussions and papers presented at a small meeting of NGOs and researchers in September 2003 which brought together experiences from the UK, Africa, and Asia to define what agencies can do to achieve education for nomadic and pastoralist children. Chapters 5–9 have been adapted from material initially commissioned as background research for the DFID policy paper 'Girls' Education: Towards a Better Future for All' (DFID 2005).Chapters 5 and 6 were adapted for the Beyond Access project by Pauline Rose and Taylor Brown from 'The Role of Capacity and Political Will in Achieving the Gender MDG'. Chapter 7 was adapted by the Beyond Access project from Debbie Budlender 'Girls' Education – the Financing Issues'. Chapter 8 and Chapter 9 were adapted for the Beyond Access project from background papers written for DFID's girls strategy paper, by Sam Gibson and Nicola Swainson, respectively (DFID 2005), with additional commissioned work by Janet Raynor for Chapter 9.

This phase of the work of Beyond Access was supported by funding from DFID. Our thanks to Rachel Hinton, Sally Gear, and Rose Kanwar from the Education and Skills Team for their collaboration and for helping us put some of our ideas of working with governments into practice. We gratefully acknowledge the guidance we received from members of the Beyond Access Advisory Committee when developing the project. Our warmest thanks to other members of Beyond Access – Chloe Challender, Amy North, Rajee Rajagopalan, and Anne Marie Peacock – for their hard work, commitment, and critical engagement with the many strands of project work. Lastly our thanks for editorial work to Catherine Robinson, who edited some of the initial papers, and to Katie Allan and the Publishing Team at Oxfam GB who have helped us to develop the initial policy papers into a book for a wider audience.

Introduction

Background

This book is designed to help non-government organisations (NGOs), practitioners, teachers, government officials, and researchers think about and develop their understanding of key issues in achieving gender equality in education. It has been compiled in order to support the development of policy and good practice for quality education for all, and to ensure that gender equality is a key part of quality education. It does this through discussions of some of the challenges to achieving gender equality in education and provides examples of initiatives in a range of contexts.

How can NGOs, practitioners, policy makers, and researchers work together so that all girls and boys have access to good-quality gender-equitable education? What would such an education look like? This book draws on the work of the Beyond Access, Gender, Education and Development project – a partnership between an NGO (Oxfam GB), a research organisation (Institute of Education, University of London), and a UK government department (the Department for International Development – DFID) – to discuss these questions and make recommendations for action. The chapters have been developed through the Beyond Access project and were published in 2005 as a series of nine separate papers in the Oxfam Programme Insights series entitled 'Education and Gender Equality'.

The first phase of the Beyond Access project (2003–2005) brought together three constituencies – policy makers, practitioners and activists, and researchers – to examine knowledge and practice regarding gender equality and education. These groups were asked to share lessons learned in order to be better able to influence the policies of government departments, national and international NGOs, and international institutions including UN agencies. Dissemination of these lessons has been achieved through various publications. Firstly, the book *Beyond Access: Transforming Policy and Practice for Gender Equality in Education* (Aikman and Unterhalter 2005) examines the extent of gender inequalities globally, the response of policy makers, and different practices addressing gender inequalities in local settings. Secondly, the papers collected in this book reflect some of the ideas that were generated between June 2003 and December 2005 through a series of seminars, workshops, and specially commissioned research. Discussions took place in the UK, Bangladesh, Kenya, South Africa, and Peru. Participants came from 35 countries and had a wide range of interests and experience. The Beyond Access project continues to disseminate learning in order to support change in practice and policy through the work of existing networks, such as the Commonwealth Education Fund, and through coalitions of NGOs, UN organisations, and policy makers at different levels of government.

This introduction serves three purposes. First, it examines the important challenges of gender parity and school completion, and gender equality and quality education which underpin the chapters of the book. It then highlights the themes running through the book and briefly summarises the content and focus of the nine chapters. Lastly it identifies developments and opportunities for taking forward a gender-equality-in-education agenda.

The challenge of gender equality

Gender parity and school completion

We live in a world in which education is characterised by extensive gender inequalities. At a time of enormously expanded access to all levels of education, of high aspirations for political participation and huge growth of knowledge economies, 77 million children are still out of school, 57 per cent of whom are girls (UNESCO 2006: 30). Seven-hundred and eighty-one million adults are illiterate and 64 per cent of these are women (UNESCO 2006: 59). Nearly one billion people, one-sixth of the world's population, have little or no education, either because they have never been to school or have had less than five years of schooling and left before acquiring key areas of knowledge and many useful skills. Two-thirds of these people are women and girls (Unterhalter 2007: 155).

The Millennium Development Goals (MDGs) were agreed in 2000 partly to address this situation, through achieving the following targets:

- MDG 2: achieve universal primary education, with the target of ensuring that all boys and girls complete a full course of primary schooling by 2015.

- MDG 3: promote gender equality and empower women, with the target of eliminating gender disparities in primary and secondary education by 2005, and in all levels of education by 2015.

In 2005 the world missed the first MDG target – gender parity in education. Gender parity means that the same proportion of girls and boys enter and complete schooling. When there is no gender parity, there is a gender gap, and a greater proportion of either boys or girls are receiving education. Based on 2003 data, UNESCO's *Global Monitoring Report* estimated that only 57 per cent of all children who enter primary school complete it (UNESCO 2006: 37). The median for Africa was 65 per cent of girls and 67 per cent of boys remaining in school until the last grade of the primary school, but in some countries, such as Mozambique and Rwanda, less than one-third of girls reach this level (UNESCO 2006: 284–5). In Africa only 21 per cent of secondary-school-age girls are in secondary school, and 26 per cent of secondary-school-age boys (UNESCO 2006: 293). In South Asia, while a higher proportion of teenagers attend secondary school, girls in school still comprise less than 50 per cent of their age group and there is a notable gender gap – 41 per cent of secondary-school-age girls are in school compared with 49 per cent of secondary-school-age boys.

There have been some encouraging moves towards increased gender parity in school, for example in Bangladesh and Malawi, where access has increased dramatically. But 'parity' is a limited goal and can mean simply measuring the changes in numbers of girls as compared with boys enrolling in school. Concern with parity may also be linked with a focus on other tangible and quantifiable factors such as the number of classrooms and toilets, numbers of textbooks and supplies of materials, and measurement of learning in terms of exam results. In places where there have been long periods of war, routinised violence, discrimination, exploitation, exclusion, and a range of different forms of poverty, achieving parity might be a substantive achievement of social justice, but parity on its own is a rather limited aspiration. A more substantive goal to aim for is quality and aspects of equality, including gender equality, in education.

Quality education and gender equality

Calculations indicate that at least one in every three girls who completes primary schooling in South Asia cannot read, write, or do arithmetic (Herz and Sperling 2004: 2). There are often concerns with quality because of large class sizes, inadequate instructional time, difficulties with the language of instruction, and the forms of assessment (UNESCO 2005). Unfortunately there is not a lot of focus on the gender inequalities embedded in these issues. There is however a growing number of predominantly small-scale qualitative studies which raise the question of gender dynamics underlying issues such as which children take most teacher time, which children succeed in examinations in more prestigious subjects, and how schools engage with issues concerning sexuality (Raynor 2005; Page 2005; Pattman and Chege 2003; Vavrus 2003; Kakuru 2006). In many countries girls are often expelled when they become pregnant, gender-based violence is inadequately tackled, and schools are ill-equipped to deal with the education of children in families affected by AIDS (Leach and Mitchell 2006).

This book, with its focus on quality and gender equality in education, raises the question of aiming for a bigger goal than gender parity or equal access to school for girls and boys – hence the phrase 'beyond access'. Although gender parity is very important, it is only one aspect of achieving a fuller sense of gender equality. The Beijing Platform for Action, adopted by the Fourth World Conference on Women in 1995, argues for the removal of deep-seated barriers to equality of opportunity for both sexes (such as discriminatory laws, customs, practices, and institutional processes) as well as developing the freedoms of all individuals, irrespective of gender, to choose and achieve outcomes they have reason to value. Oxfam believes that the right to education is a social and economic right. Education can help to overcome constraints on capabilities partly through developing the knowledge, understanding, and skills that all girls and boys, women and men need in order to achieve what they value for their lives. This means ensuring an education system which allows all individuals, irrespective of gender, to develop their capabilities and freedoms. Some aspects of this equality are the freedom to attend school, to learn and participate there in safety and security, to develop identities that tolerate others, and to enjoy a range of economic, political, and cultural opportunities and valued outcomes. These and other issues are explored in the chapters of this book. The conclusion provides recommendations for actions to be taken by government, donors, and civil society.

The focus of the book

There are five themes which thread through the book and shape its overall agenda for gender equality in education:

- Partnerships between practitioners, policy makers and researchers

- Multiple interventions and actions

- Advocacy for policy and practice change

- Government commitment to and responsibility for basic education

- Adequate and sustainable financing.

Partnerships to achieve a global development agenda. There is an urgent sense that the MDGs can only be achieved when different sectors and constituencies work together. There are different kinds of partnerships aimed at improving girls' education. Some are high-profile partnerships – that is high status, high visibility, and wide geographical spread – such as the Global Campaign for Education (GCE) and the Forum for African Women Educationalists (FAWE). There are also partnerships at the national level – such as education coalitions – which bring together NGOs, community-based organisations, and teacher unions (such as TEN-MET in Tanzania and the Ghana National Education Campaign Coalition GNECC – see Smyth and Rao 2005). Partnerships for gender equality can be focused on a common goal – to achieve MDG 3 and education for all (EFA[1]) at the Jomtein conference. A subsequent meeting at the Education Forum at Dakar in 2000 led to a larger government and NGO engagement to work on EFA. They can also be focused on the process – working in a gender sensitive way to achieve these goals.

Multiple interventions and actions to achieve sustainable change. Firstly there need to be specific *interventions* to overcome well-documented barriers to access and participation for girls and boys. Such interventions might include policy or legislation to remove school fees or provide water and latrines. Secondly there is a need for *institutional* changes, such as reform of teacher-training courses to increase gender awareness, or institutionalising systems for gender mainstreaming, in budgeting or planning. These changes can help to build more positive social relations in schools and education departments. Thirdly there should be *interactive* processes that build, maintain, and critique connections between those working on gender in different kinds of organisations – schools, NGOs, governments, inter-government organisations, and universities. All three forms of action are necessary to help support change for gender equality in education (Unterhalter 2007).

Advocacy for policy and practice change and to achieve financial targets. 'Doing advocacy' can involve lobbying decision-makers, community mobilisation, mass communication campaigns and media work, or organising public demonstrations. Advocacy messages based on good-quality evidence from practice and lessons learned are important ways of influencing decision makers and transforming public perceptions, behaviour, and attitudes. Too often gender is left out of the streamlined messages of advocacy campaigns, but work in the Beyond Access project on media messages shows very practically how this can be included (North 2006).

Government commitment to and responsibility for basic education. There is evidence today that only governments can work at the scale necessary to provide universal access to education and ensure the right of all children (especially the marginalised and poor) to an education which is free and of good quality (Oxfam International 2006a). Clearly, civil-society organisations and private companies also have a role to play, but this must be in the context of a strong government system that can regulate and integrate them into public systems. Civil-society organisations often provide educational services where there is excess demand and there is no state alternative. They can also develop and lead on innovative approaches to education and are important in working as forums that oversee the work of government and strengthen processes of accountability.

Adequate and sustainable financing for gender-equitable education. Spending on education has been rising in most countries over the past decade, and around half of African countries are now spending a higher percentage of their budget on education than are high-income countries in North America and Europe. However, Oxfam's report 'In the Public Interest' (Oxfam International 2006a) states that, globally, up to $17bn extra per year is still needed to put every child in a decent primary school – of which at least $10bn will need to come from rich countries by 2010.

Overview of the chapters

Chapter 1: **Beyond access for girls and boys** frames the issues and challenges involved in achieving gender equality and quality education for all. The issues include not only ensuring access to education for girls and women, but also the completion of a good quality education for both boys and girls. This chapter considers the way in which terms such as gender mainstreaming and gender equality and equity are used and discusses why, within a gender approach, focusing on girls and women is important. It also looks at the role of boys and men in challenging and changing unequal gender relations. This chapter and the following two chapters were developed from papers and discussion at four seminars sponsored by the Beyond Access project focusing on:

- Partnerships for Gender Equality and Quality Basic Education in Schools

- Developing Gender Equality in Adult Education

- Pedagogic Strategies for Gender Equality and Quality Basic Education in Schools

- Curriculum for Gender Equality and Quality Basic Education in Schools

Individual papers were commissioned for these seminars and policy papers were drafted on the basis of the discussions.

Chapter 2: **Gender equality in schools** explores gender equality within the school, examining the curriculum in terms of rights, decision-making processes, and social relations. It also investigates teaching and learning strategies and the different dimensions of a gender-equitable approach to schooling. These include thinking not only about how teachers can teach 'gender equality', but also how they live it both in the school and in their private lives.

Chapter 3: **Gender equality and adult basic education** recognises the power struggles between different political agendas that result in little or no education for marginalised adults. To be effective, adult basic education and literacy policies and programmes must also be sensitive to a broad range of urgent issues such as HIV and AIDS, violence and conflict, poverty and discrimination. In a field marked by the diversity of providers, funding sources, programme aims, and learners' aims and goals, the chapter looks at what needs to happen for adult basic education to transform the situation of women and men.

Chapter 4: **Beyond the mainstream** takes the example of education for nomadic and pastoralist girls and boys to examine the challenges in achieving gender equality among those who are beyond the reach of mainstream, formal education. It raises the question of both demand and supply: what do pastoralist and nomadic girls and boys want from formal education, which mostly ignores or denies their indigenous knowledge, skills, and practices? And how flexible and gender-aware are the policies and the delivery mechanisms of ministries of education and other implementers? This chapter was developed from discussions and papers presented at a small meeting of NGOs and researchers in 2003. This meeting brought together experiences from the UK, Africa, and Asia to define what agencies can do to achieve EFA for nomadic and pastoralist children. The chapter was enriched by examples from programmes being carried out by Oxfam GB and partners in sub-Saharan Africa.

Chapter 5: **Making it happen** and Chapter 6: **Developing capacity to achieve gender equality in education** examine the role of capacity building and political will (commitment, leadership, and responsiveness) in achieving MDGs 2 and 3. They look at processes of change rather than specific policy shifts and together illustrate how different forms of capacity – individual, organisational, and institutional – are needed for strong gender-sensitive policies and strategies. These chapters were adapted for the Beyond Access project by Pauline Rose and Taylor Brown from 'The Role of Capacity and Political Will in Achieving the Gender MDG', a background paper for *Girls' Education: Towards a Better Future for All*, (DFID 2005).

Chapter 7: **Gender-responsive budgeting in education** provides an introduction to what gender-responsive budgeting is and what it can tell us. Through examples from around the world, it illustrates how gender-responsive budgeting can be used to investigate the impact of a government budget and the policies and programmes that it funds, on women and men, boys and girls – and how this information can be used to promote gender equality in education through sound financial decision-making. This chapter was adapted for the Beyond Access project by Debbie Budlender from 'Girls' Education – the Financing Issues', a background paper for *Girls' Education: Towards a Better Future for All*, (DFID 2005).

Chapter 8: **Girls' education in Africa** and Chapter 9: **Girls' education in South Asia** were also adapted for the Beyond Access project from background papers written for DFID's girls strategy paper, by Sam Gibson and Nicola Swainson, respectively (DFID 2005), with additional commissioned work by Janet Raynor for Chapter 9. These are overview papers intended to provide a balanced reflection of what is known about girls' enrolment, progression, and completion in primary and secondary schooling in Africa and South Asia. Literature reviews show that a considerable amount of experience has been accumulated on girls' education in both sub-Saharan Africa and South Asia. Consequently, these chapters provide a snapshot and highlight some of the factors that make Africa distinct from South Asia and vice-versa.

Looking ahead

The achievements since the beginning of 2005

The chapters of this book were first published as papers in 2005, the year the target for MDG3 on gender parity in primary and secondary education was meant to be achieved; a year when world leaders were called upon to take drastic action to act to meet the target and show that girls' education matters. By the end of 2005 it was clear that the MDG target had not been met in 94 out of 187 countries for which there was data. And meeting the wider goals concerned with quality and equality was still a very long way off.

In 2005 36 million people in over 70 countries united under the Global Call to Action against Poverty, and demanded that the world's leaders act, in the words of Nelson Mandela, to overcome the injustice of global poverty. They demanded that leaders deliver debt cancellation, more and better aid, and trade justice. Leaders at the G8 Summit at Gleneagles promised to increase aid by $50bn annually by 2010, which could, among other things, pay for every child to go to school. Those leaders made strong statements about the importance of free, compulsory, good quality primary education for all and also of the Fast Track Initiative (FTI), a global aid mechanism. The UK government has played a critical leadership role in increasing aid to Africa, securing new international commitments for more aid to education, and increasing its own aid to the FTI. The FTI review of progress in September 2006 reported that 20 countries had developed education plans that could secure them funding through the FTI; 12 more were expected to have plans endorsed for funding by the end of 2006; and 27 countries had expressed an interest in joining the FTI process (FTI 2006).

Debt cancellation is already beginning to make a difference, for example in Zambia where extra funds will be put towards the recruitment of more than 4,500 teachers and the rehabilitation of schools in rural and urban areas (Oxfam 2006b). But while debt cancellation is starting to be delivered, the growth in aid in key G8 nations is not enough to meet the promises made at Gleneagles and the increases will still come too late and fall far short of UN and World Bank estimates of what is needed to meet the MDGs.

Increasing flows of resources into education have not been matched by increasing concerns for practices to develop gender equality in education. There is huge variation in the quality of gender analysis which countries have undertaken to qualify for FTI support and, while most countries collect some gender-disaggregated data and have objectives to improve girls' enrolments, only four countries had developed plans on the basis of a broader concept of gender equality and only Ghana had made a commitment to mainstream concerns with gender (Seel and Clarke 2005). But at the end of 2005 the FTI meeting in Beijing agreed to revisit the FTI goals to include an explicit commitment to gender, and to strengthen its appraisal guidelines to highlight that gender cannot be sidelined, and close monitoring is needed (Seel and Clarke 2005). So while changes at the FTI indicate that some steps have been taken to move gender equality in education further, the agenda is proceeding slowly, and action within countries is often limited and unsupported.

The UN Girls' Education Initiative (UNGEI) was launched in 2000 to take forward the vision of gender equality in education outlined at the World Education Forum in Dakar (2000). In 2005 UNGEI began a reassessment of its way of working and started to build conditions to support work on gender and education at the country level (UNGEI 2006). Discussions on the reform of the UN, which began in 2005, may offer some scope for strengthening the UNGEI partnership.

The Global Campaign for Education (GCE) issued a forthright statement when the MDG target for 2005 was not met, highlighting how this was a 'tragedy for those left behind' and a health warning for the whole MDG project (GCE 2005). GCE continues to raise issues concerning gender discrimination in education and the human-rights abuses this implies. A number of regional networks and partnerships promote gender equality (such as the Asian gender focal points working in ministries of education, or broader coalitions, such as the Asian South Pacific Bureau for Adult Education). These networks have long given attention to issues of inequality and empowerment. At the national level, for example, gender and education activists in Kenya have had a high profile through the education NGO coalition Elimu Yetu ('Our Education'). However, discussions inside teachers' organisations about gender issues are generally muted, and the EFA movement has not succeeded in building links with the wider women's movement which campaigned vociferously through 2005 on aid, the destructive effects of economic policies, and the continuing high levels of violence against women (Unterhalter 2007).

What more needs to be done?

While some important steps have been taken, there is now urgency for action and change. There is urgency to achieve the EFA goals and meet the MDG 2015 targets, urgency because of the need to recognise the role which education is seen to play in HIV prevention, and urgency because the expansion of access to school has not been met by equivalent gains in overcoming illiteracy.

Gender inequality in society is a huge issue that cannot be tackled by education alone. However, **education systems and schools can contribute to gender equality rather than sustaining inequalities.** Areas of fruitful action include curriculum change, tackling sexual harassment in and around school, the training of gender-sensitive teachers, and attention to diverse learning styles. Initiatives like these often remain small-scale, but when initiatives are institutionalised, well-resourced, and incorporated into long-term policy visions, the potential exists for schools to become a beacon and model for wider societal changes (Subrahmanian 2005). Making connections between different initiatives and sustaining work that has already been done remains a huge challenge.

It is particularly important to encourage public demand and government commitment to go beyond primary schooling. The concept of EFA elaborated at Dakar is much broader than the policy goals underpinning MDGs 2 and 3, which are concerned mainly with primary schooling. EFA contained *a vision for adult education* and an idea that education entailed learning in many contexts, not just at school. However, there is much less dynamism and funding linked to institutionalising change for adult education than there is for delivering primary schooling. UNESCO plans to convene its sixth conference on adult education in 2009 and will stress the crucial role of this sector in supporting the achievement of all the MDGs as well as EFA. There is a compelling need to draw out the gender issues this raises.

As larger numbers of girls and boys gain access to and complete primary schooling a further challenge is to provide *good quality secondary schooling* and ensure this too is gender-equitable. In many countries girls leave school in the final years of the primary cycle and families find it too costly to support their study at secondary level. Yet studies suggest that girls with some years of secondary schooling are better able to use what they have learned than those with only primary schooling and that post-primary education provides girls with the greater benefits (Grown *et al.* 2005). Initiatives such as stipend schemes that support girls to go to secondary school need to be broadened to ensure that all children can continue their education beyond primary school. There also needs to be consideration and attention to some of the gender questions of access, progression, and quality at this level.

The *changing approach to aid delivery*, with bilateral donors increasingly favouring sector support or direct budget support, holds out the potential to improve conditions for the institutionalisation of change. Gender budgeting is a means of ensuring that funding to education promotes gender equality. To date, the few gender-budgeting exercises that have been undertaken are at the national level and have not addressed adult education, concern with the most marginalised and excluded, and processes of local participation in decision-making.

Aid and financing of education are clearly important resources for gender equality and quality education, but more needs to be done to clarify *how resources are developed, planned, and used* to achieve gender-equitable education. People are a key resource; for example qualified, knowledgeable, and able teachers, administrators, and members of school management committees. Civil society is a key resource for holding government and private organisations accountable for the delivery of gender-equitable education.

In many countries women's organisations, and organisations representing the poorest parents, remain excluded from participating in the work of school management. Where there have been concerted efforts to *work with women's organisations*, for example in Uganda, India, and some provinces of Pakistan, huge achievements have been noted in terms of promoting women's voices (Subrahmanian 2005). There has also been considerable success with projects that take time to work with traditional leaders and overcome hostilities and prejudice (Unterhalter *et al.* 2005). But in order to enhance this work, much more needs to be understood about the gendered nature of organisations, and the ways in which different women contribute to civic life. Lessons from the 1990s about gender training and organisational development have much to contribute to developing mobilisation for gender equality in education.

The *HIV and AIDS pandemic* presents a further enormous challenge to putting in place gender-equitable education. Fifty-seven per cent of people infected with HIV in sub-Saharan Africa are women. By the end of 2003, some 17 million women were living with HIV in this region. During the early years of the epidemic, infection was most prevalent amongst men, but the burden of infection among girls and young women is growing, to the extent that we can talk of the 'feminisation' of the epidemic. In Southern Africa, young women are two to seven times more likely to be infected with HIV than young men (Hargreaves and Boler 2006). Today rigorous reviews of research suggest there seems to be a direct correlation between completion of primary schooling and reduction in HIV infection rates, as more highly educated girls and women are better able to negotiate safer sex and reduce HIV rates. This is attributed to the indirect influence of education through equipping young people with cognitive skills and boosting self-confidence and status; through providing young people with skills and knowledge to be productive members of well functioning societies; and also through a more direct role in teaching about HIV prevention and AIDS (Hargreaves and Boler 2006).

But what kinds of teaching best support programmes in HIV prevention? It is not yet well understood how teachers can be supported to teach about HIV and AIDS, and the ways in which this work can be used to engage with views about gender equality. The difficulties of working on gender equality and HIV with teachers has been documented (Thorpe 2005; Bhana *et al.* 2006; Kakuru 2006). The complex issues this work raises about teachers' identities and the ways in which gender, sexuality, and socio-economic inequality connect indicate a need to think about new forms of action in schools in response to the epidemic. Cultural practices and social relations continue to disempower girls and women and make them vulnerable to HIV. We need to know more about what kind of education and what kinds of teachers and training are needed to meet the challenge of HIV and AIDS.

This book is not intended to be an exhaustive exploration of gender equality in education. Indeed, there are several important areas that are not dealt with in detail such as education and gender in the context of conflict, the education response to the HIV and AIDS pandemic, or the ways in which schooling might mitigate some of the most harmful effects of climate change (indeed, though acknowledged as one of the most important development challenges today, the gendered effects of climate change are poorly understood at present). The book is not, then, an attempt to provide a comprehensive plan of action for working on gender issues but, rather, teases out the gender-equality implications for some key areas of education for all.

Sheila Aikman and Elaine Unterhalter

References

Aikman, S. and Unterhalter, E. (eds.) (2005) *Beyond Access: Transforming policy and practice for gender equality in education*, Oxford: Oxfam.

Bhana, D., Morrell, R., Epstein, D., and Moletsane, R. (2006) 'The hidden work of caring: teachers and the maturing AIDS epidemic in diverse secondary schools in Durban', *Journal of Education* 38: 5–20.

Fast Track Initiative Development Committee (2006) 'Progress Report for the Education for All Fast Track Initiative', Washington: World Bank, available at
http://siteresources.worldbank.org/DEVCOMMINT/Documentation/2104
6513/DC2006-0015(E)-Education.pdf, last accessed January 2007.

Global Campaign for Education (2005) 'UN Millennium Summit delivers rhetoric without commitment', Johannesburg: Global Campaign for Education, available at
http://www.campaignforeducation.org/news/2005/news_past_sep05.html, last accessed December 2006.

Grown, C., Das Gupta, G., and Kes, A. (2005) 'Taking Action: Achieving Gender Equality and Empowering Women', UN Millennium Project, Task Force on Education and Gender Equality, London: Earthscan.

Hargreaves, J. and Boler, T. (2006) *Girl Power: The impact of girls' education on HIV and sexual behaviour*, Johannesburg: ActionAid.

Herz, G. and Sperling, B. (2004) *What works in Girls' Education: Evidence and Policies from the Developing World*, Council on Foreign Relations.

International Monetary Fund World Bank Group (2006), 'Special Ministerial Roundtable on Education Report of Proceedings', available at: http://www1.worldbank.org/education/efafti/documents/TranscriptRound tableSept2006.pdf, last accessed January 2007.

Kakuru, D. M. (2006) *The Combat for Gender Equlity in Education: Rural livelihood pathways in the context of HIV/AIDS,* Wageningen: Wageningen Academic Publishers.

Leach, F. and Mitchell, C. (2006) 'Situating the study of gender violence in and around schools', in F. Leach and C. Mitchell (eds.) *Combating Gender Violence in Schools,* Stoke on Trent: Trentham Books.

North, A. (2006) *Working with Gender and the Media: A guide for training and planning,* Oxford: Oxfam.

Oxfam International (2006a) 'In the Public Interest – Health, Education, and Water and Sanitation for All', Oxford: Oxfam International.

Oxfam International (2006b) 'The View from the Summit – Gleneagles G8 one year on', Oxford: Oxfam.

Page, E. (2005) 'Gender and the construction of identitites in Indian elementary education', unpublished Ph.D thesis, Institute of Education, University of London.

Pattman, R. and Chege, F. (2003), *Finding our voices: Gendered and sexual identities and HIV/AIDS in education,* Nairobi: UNICEF.

Raynor, J. (2005) 'Educating girls in Bangladesh: watering a neighbour's tree?', in S. Aikman and E. Unterhalter (eds.), Oxford: Oxfam: 83–105.

Seel, A. and Clarke, D. (2005) *Integrating gender into education for all: Fast Track Initiative processes and national education plans,* New York: UNGEI.

Smyth, I. and Rao, N. (eds.) (2005) *Partnerships for Girls' Education,* Oxford: Oxfam.

Subrahmanian, R. (2004) 'The Politics of Resourcing Education: A Review of New Aid Modalities from a Gender Perspective', paper presented at Beyond Access seminar 3, available at http://www.ioe.ac.uk/schools/efps/GenderEducDev/Ramya%20paper.pdf, last accessed December 2006.

Thorpe, M. (2005) 'Learning about HIV/AIDS in schools: does a gender-equality approach make a difference?', in S. Aikman, S. and E. Unterhalter (eds.), Oxford: Oxfam: 199–211.

UNESCO (2006) *Literacy for Life*, Global Monitoring Report, Paris: UNESCO.

UNESCO (2005) *The Quality Imperative*, Global Monitoring Report, Paris: UNESCO.

UNGEI (2005) 'Integrating gender into FTI processes and tools', paper prepared for the FTI meeting, Cairo, November, available at: http://www.fasttrackinitiative.org/education/efafti/documents/Cairo/ Background%20Documents/Integrating_Gender_into_FTI.pdf, accessed February 2007.

UNGEI (2006) 'Ungei country sheet. Review of UNGEI activities', New York: UNGEI, available at: http://www.ungei.org/resources/files/UNGEI_country_sheet.pdf, accessed February 2007.

Unterhalter, E. (2007) *Gender, Schooling and Global Social Justice*, Abingdon: Routledge.

Unterhalter, E., Challender, C., and Rajagopalan, R. (2005) 'Measuring gender equality in education', in S. Aikman and E. Unterhalter (eds.), Oxford: Oxfam: 60–81.

Vavrus, F. (2003) *Desire and Decline: Schooling amid crisis in Tanzania*, New York: Peter Lang.

Note

1   The Education for All movement is a global network of governments, international NGOs, and NGOs working to provide quality basic education for all children, youth, and adults. The movement was launched at the World Conference on Education for All in 1990.

1. Beyond access for girls and boys

How to achieve good quality, gender-equitable education

This chapter frames the issues and challenges to be faced in achieving gender equality and quality Education For All (EFA). The issues – which include not only ensuring access to education for girls and women, but the completion of a good quality education for both boys and girls so that they can use their education to have a positive effect on their futures – are taken up in more detail in subsequent chapters.

Why is gender equality important, and why are we still talking mostly about girls and women?

Key facts and figures

- There are approximately 100 million school-age children worldwide who are not in school. Of these, 55 per cent are girls.

- There are almost 800 million people aged 15 and above living without basic literacy skills worldwide, of whom 64 per cent are women.[1]

- Of 180 countries that have been monitoring progress towards gender parity in education, 76 have not yet achieved equal numbers of girls and boys in primary school, and the gender disparities are nearly always at the expense of girls.[2]

- In some countries, girls outperform boys in school, but later fail to gain equality in work or political participation. In the poorest countries it is girls who face barriers to equality of opportunity, and do not achieve equal outcomes from education.

- Education is a right. Girls who are not in school and women who are illiterate are being denied their right to an education.

Education and the Millennium Development Goals

The United Nations' eight Millennium Development Goals (MDGs), aimed at eradicating global poverty and promoting development, are among the most widely supported set of global aspirations in effect today. All 191 member states of the UN have pledged their commitment to meet them by 2015.

Two of the MDGs directly address issues of education and gender:

- Goal 2 aims to 'achieve universal primary education', with a specific target to 'ensure that all boys and girls complete a full course of primary schooling'.

- Goal 3 is broadly framed to 'promote gender equality and empower women', with a narrow target to 'eliminate gender disparity in primary and secondary education preferably by 2005 and at all levels by 2015'.[3]

The MDGs focus on the number of girls and boys enrolling in, or finishing, school as a measurement of success, but this is a very crude measure of gender equality and empowerment. Gender parity simply refers to equal numbers of boys and girls being present in schooling.

More ambitious and meaningful aims would be that, once in school, girls and boys experience quality learning and teaching, and that equality in schooling is linked with positive changes towards equality in broader society. Yet measures and actions for ensuring the quality of education and achieving gender equity in education are not addressed explicitly in any of the MDGs. The Millennium targets and goals need to be widened to address this aim and should include, as well as the numbers of children not in school, the high drop-out rates, and the numbers of girls and boys who complete primary schooling but who are still unable to read, write, calculate, or use their learning. If many of the MDGs are to be achieved, the current focus on access of girls to education must also be linked with a broader focus on adult education and literacy for women (see Chapter 3).

Culture within schools

Millions of girls who attend school today are the first in their families ever to do so. Success in getting girls into school may be sustained if schools are made welcoming for them, with positive changes in approaches to learning and teaching and in the curriculum. Without this, although larger numbers of children will enter school, many of them will quickly drop out again, and of those who stay, only some will learn in ways that will help them to thrive.

Both teachers and pupils often have very set ideas about the ways in which girls and boys should behave, and the organisation of the school day can reinforce these ideas. Chores such as fetching water, cleaning classrooms, and cooking for a male head teacher are often assigned to girls and female teachers. Some teachers have deep-seated beliefs that boys are naturally superior to girls, that they perform better than girls, and that a woman or girl should not challenge male authority. These beliefs can result in girls not achieving to their best potential and can restrict their aspirations for further study. Harassment of girls by male teachers is a major reason for girls dropping out of school.

Box 1.1 Making schooling safer in Bangladesh

By the late 1990s in Bangladesh, national statistics indicated that equal numbers of boys and girls were enrolling in both primary and lower secondary schooling. However, there is still a long way to go to achieve gender equality. Insecurity is a major factor constraining girls' education, and every day schoolgirls run the risk of experiencing violent behaviour.

This has not gone unchallenged, and a variety of projects address the root causes of sexual violence, mostly through NGOs. These include the Centre for Mass Education and Science and the Bangladesh Rural Advancement Committee (BRAC), which runs workshops with adolescent girls – and now also boys – through the Adolescent Peer Organised Network. While promising, however, such programmes are only able to reach a small part of the population.

Other projects tend to focus on the logistical aspects of making access to school safer for girls – for example, by building schools within a 'safe' walking distance of their homes. While such measures may be a useful stopgap, it is necessary to move the focus beyond the concrete resources needed to get girls into school and to address the hostile environment they face while at school, and the wider societal issues of sexual violence.[4]

Teacher conditions and retention

In many countries, retention of teachers is difficult, especially in rural areas. Teachers face multiple problems, including low pay and poor conditions, that contribute to low morale and low status. Poor mobility and transport mean that often they receive no professional support in their classrooms.

Payment of their salaries can be a problem if the government has decentralised responsibility for payment, and local authorities do not have adequate funding or efficient systems for payment. Worse still, where there is no government schooling, it is often the poorest communities who have to run their own schools and pay for their own teachers' salaries.

Women teachers often have even lower pay and even fewer opportunities for promotion than men. Employment of women as 'para-teachers', at a fraction of the salary of a regular teacher, has serious implications for the professionalism and status of women. In some countries, women also have inadequate arrangements for maternity leave. However, teachers can help to make schools transformative places by helping girls and boys challenge gender stereotypes and inequalities, both in the school and outside. For this they themselves need training and support (see Chapter 2).

Wider society

To increase demand for girls' education, it is important that it is seen as valuable and relevant. What women and girls *want* from their education depends on how they feel it will help them in the future. Some people refuse to contemplate the education of girls because it appears to undermine accepted cultural practices. It is important not to ignore opposition to gender equality in school but to consider instead how the race and class inequalities that sometimes nurture this opposition can be addressed. When traditional leaders and elders have been consulted, there has been success in changing attitudes to formal schooling for girls. However, *all* views in communities including those of women need to be taken into account, not just those of the recognised leader or head of household.

Government responsibilities

Education, in the most rounded sense, is an individual, a community, and a household issue, but the state has an overall responsibility to ensure formal education is provided equitably to all children (see Chapter 5). Basic education should be free at the point of delivery, because charges are inequitable, whether user fees or 'hidden' expenses, such as transport, books, uniforms, or community levies.

Chapter 4 looks at the example of nomad and pastoralist children, who form a significant minority of those out of school, and considers how, if the MDGs are to be achieved, governments must develop flexible and innovative strategies to reach them, help close the gender gaps, and support quality education.

Partnership

The notion of 'partnership', involving greater co-ordination and harmonisation at all levels to achieve a global development agenda, underlies all the MDGs. Examples of the different kinds of partnership that have been set up with the aim of working explicitly for girls' education and gender equality, include the Beyond Access project, the Global Campaign for Education (GCE),[5] and the Forum for African Women Educationalists (FAWE).[6] An example of a high-profile partnership between UN agencies and donors is the UNICEF-led UN Girls' Education Initiative (UNGEI).[7]

The challenge is to develop new and innovative partnerships based on equality, trust, respect, and dialogue, where the agenda is set jointly and local views and knowledge are respected and deliberately sought. Through such partnerships, people excluded by poverty, discrimination, and HIV and AIDS can influence and control aspects of their lives, using institutions, opportunities, and strategies that they shape for themselves. Good communication and dialogue, with flexible, transparent processes, where disagreements are negotiated and resolved, are essential characteristics in developing such partnerships.

Partnership needs to be approached in two complementary ways to achieve gender equality in education, and therefore to attain the MDGs:

• Through a common goal to achieve MDG 3 and Education for All.

• Through working in a gender-equitable way to achieve all the goals.

Commitment at international, national, and local levels is needed to build partnerships to achieve this, along with greater participation at the local, school, and community levels.

HIV and AIDS

Gender inequality is a major driver of the HIV pandemic. Gender disparities in education are particularly significant, because they contribute to the social conditions that facilitate the spread of the HIV virus. There were an estimated 40 million people worldwide living with HIV. In recent years, the overall proportion of HIV-positive women has steadily increased and the epidemic's 'feminisation' is most apparent in sub-Saharan Africa, where 57 per cent of adults infected are women, and 75 per cent of young people infected are women and girls.[8] To date, education planning which takes into consideration HIV and AIDS has still to adopt a comprehensive approach to gender and to addressing gender equality.

While it is extremely important to promote the education of girls, the development needs of boys should also be addressed. Change will not happen until both girls and boys change sexual and reproductive behaviour and gender norms. Harmful practices, such as violence against girls at school and the sexual abuse of girls by teachers, need to be eliminated. This can be done by ensuring that schools become environments where gender equality is practised openly and consistently – including the removal of stereotyping and gender bias in the curriculum. Teachers can be trained in making the classroom a more positive environment for girls in terms of layout, use of resources, and teacher-student interaction. At the same time, ministries of education need to monitor and evaluate the implementation of education policy from a gender-equality perspective and take action to ensure that HIV prevention and the impact of AIDS are addressed through education.[9]

Evidence strongly suggests that policy and programme interventions that serve to promote gender equality at school will contribute to reducing the vulnerability of young people, girls and women in particular, to HIV infection. Work not explicitly focused on AIDS – such as advocacy work for the abolition of fees and the protection of girls at and around school from violence, exploitation, and discrimination – can directly and strategically contribute to national HIV and AIDS responses.

Box 1.2 Developing a gender-equality approach to working with HIV and AIDS

In 2001–2003, building on experiences in South Africa, the Juventude Alerta (Youth Alert) programme at the teacher training college in Beira, Mozambique, trained volunteer teachers in participatory techniques and activities aimed at engaging teenage students in rural secondary schools on issues surrounding HIV, including gender issues.

A volunteer teacher started a group for the older girls in her class, to look at issues important to them as young women. The girls were eager to discuss, and begin to assert, their sexual rights. Three weeks on, the school principal spoke with the volunteer teacher. 'We like what you are doing, encouraging these girls to work harder and be good, but please be careful, we don't want them having the idea that they cannot be cooks and cleaners of the house…They must know their place…,' he said. This illustrates the difficulties encountered by the programme, which actively sought to challenge male power in heterosexual relationships and to teach how this issue needed to be carefully and sensitively addressed.[10]

What do we mean by 'gender equality' and 'quality education'?

Key terms in common use when talking about education include 'gender parity', 'gender equality', and 'gender equity'. This section provides an easy guide to how these terms are generally used.

Gender parity in education is a rather narrow aspiration, simply entailing equal numbers of girls and boys being present in schools. Many countries are making progress on gender parity, but the limited nature of the concept means that more challenging dimensions of gender equality and equity are not being monitored, measured or discussed.

Gender equality and gender equity: there is no consensus as to the precise difference between these two terms, exactly what they mean, or how they should be used. They are often used interchangeably. However, it is generally agreed that to achieve gender equity/equality, there is a need to remove deep-seated barriers to equality of opportunity for both sexes – such as discriminatory laws, customs, practices, and institutional processes. This process of working towards equality is sometimes called practicing equity. It also entails developing the freedoms of all individuals, irrespective of gender, to choose outcomes they value.

Gender mainstreaming seeks to ensure that organisations and institutions express gender equality as one of their aims and that they actively promote it in their work. There is a lack of emphasis in the education sector on gender analysis, gender training, capacity building, and networking to redress gender inequalities. This is what mainstreaming should be about.

Quality education: an education system lacks key dimensions of quality if it is discriminatory or does not ensure that the education of all girls and boys is personally and socially worthwhile. Dimensions of educational quality which are crucial for the achievement of gender equality in schooling include the content of learning materials and the curriculum, the nature of the teaching and learning materials, teacher-pupil relations, and gender-sensitive use of resources. Aspects of quality and gender equality in education include the freedom to enter school, to learn and participate there in safety and security, to develop identities that tolerate others, to promote health, and to enjoy economic, political, and cultural opportunities.

What is needed to move towards good quality, gender-equitable education for all?

Key points

• Adequate resources: financial and human (see Chapter 7).

• Increased individual, institutional, and organisational capacity to deliver gender equality in education (see Chapter 6).

• Participation by NGOs, community-based organisations, teachers, parents, and students themselves, especially girls and women.

• Networking and partnerships between organisations for greater impact on change.

• Good documentation of what works and what does not work, and why.

Key processes and organisations

Education for All

The Framework for Action, formulated at the World Education Forum in Dakar, Senegal in 2000, reaffirmed the commitment of governments to EFA by 2015. UNESCO chairs the High Level Group on EFA, monitors progress towards it at the Institute for Statistics, and produces annual Global Monitoring Reports. UNICEF is the lead agency for the UN Girls' Education Initiative (UNGEI), launched at Dakar in 2000, which aims to eliminate gender discrimination and disparity in education systems, through action at global, national, district, and community levels.

Gender equality

Under the auspices of the Commission for the Status of Women, the Fourth World Conference on Women, held in Beijing in 1995, agreed a 'Platform for Action' based on seven main points, including protection against violence and the promotion of economic autonomy for women. Inequalities and inadequacies in education and training, and unequal access to them, are critical areas of concern. In 2005, a 'Beijing +10' review and appraisal of progress on the Platform for Action was held in New York.

Human development and ending poverty

At the UN Millennium Summit in 2000, 150 heads of state adopted the United Nations Millennium Declaration and resolved to meet eight MDGs by 2015. These include halving the proportion of people living in poverty and ensuring primary education for all children. Progress on the eight MDGs was reviewed in New York in September 2005. The Global Call to Action against Poverty was launched in 2005, as an international movement seeking to hold governments accountable for their promises on ending poverty.[11]

Civil society campaigning for EFA

The Global Campaign for Education (GCE) brings together major NGOs and teachers' unions in over 150 countries around the world. It lobbies the international community to fulfil its promises to provide free, compulsory public basic education for all, and in particular for disadvantaged and deprived sections of society. The GCE-sponsored Global Week of Action, held in April each year, promotes education as a basic human right. The Forum for African Women Educationalists (FAWE) was created in 1992 and has grown into a network of 33 national chapters across Africa. FAWE seeks to ensure that girls have access to school, complete their studies, and perform well at all levels.

Notes

1   UNESCO (2004) 'Education For All – The Quality Imperative' EFA Global Monitoring Report 2005, Paris: UNESCO.

2   UNESCO (2005) 'Education for All – Literacy for Life', EFA Global Monitoring Report 2006, Paris: UNESCO.

3   http://www.un.org/millenniumgoals. The MDG3 target of gender parity by 2005 has already been missed.

4   J. Raynor (2003) 'Girls Running the Gauntlet', Equals, Issue 3, October 2003.

5   http://www.campaignforeducation.org.

6   http://www.fawe.org.

7   http://www.ungei.org.

8   UNAIDS (2004) '2004 Report on the Global AIDS Epidemic', Geneva: UNAIDS.

9   D. Clarke (2005) 'Planning and Evaluation for Gender Equality in Education in the context of HIV and AIDS', Beyond Access Seminar 5.

10 M. Thorpe (2005) 'Learning About HIV/AIDS in Schools: Does a Gender Equality Approach Make a Difference?', In S. Aikman and E. Unterhalter (eds.).

11 http://www.whiteband.org.

2. Gender equality in schools

This chapter discusses the content and delivery of education and how it can reflect and reproduce gender inequalities. Girls' and boys' learning and interaction with each other, and the teacher, are influenced by ways of teaching, the content of the curriculum, and relations within the classroom. The chapter considers these aspects of education provision – curriculum, teaching and learning, and the dynamics of the classroom and school. It recommends changes needed to ensure that education provision will promote gender equality.

Gender equality in schools: the curriculum teaching, and gender equality

Education for All (EFA) means enrolling and retaining all girls and boys in school. It is also about ensuring that girls and women of all ages develop their full potential through education and are able to ensure their full and equal participation in building a better world.

For many girls, gender inequality is a feature both of their lives and of their experience of education. Gender equality in teaching is a central component of a good-quality education. To increase equality of access to education, and to sustain progress towards Education For All, it is necessary to develop teaching methods, new ways of learning, and curricula that enable girls and boys to participate in learning as equals. The culture of a school and its practices outside of formal lessons, for example, in the playground or during meal times, also affect how girls and boys learn. So gender equality needs to be a central part of the development of the school curriculum and ways of teaching.

Children will want to come to school and will enjoy the experience of learning if schools implement good-quality gender-equitable curricula, and ways of teaching. Governments have a responsibility to develop gender-equitable education policies for children's learning, as well as for their long-term well-being.

What is 'the curriculum'?

The *Oxford English Dictionary* defines the curriculum as 'the subjects comprising a course of study in a school or college'. It reflects the knowledge that society considers valuable and appropriate to be taught in schools. As society changes, the curriculum will also change, as will the way in which it is viewed and what is considered valuable. This means that the curriculum, and teaching practices, can express ideas about gender equality, or can reproduce ideas and practices marked by gender inequality. Teaching and learning materials, evaluation and assessment procedures, and language policy are also components of the curriculum.

Over the past ten years there has been a great deal of curriculum reform as states reassess their national identity or their position in the global economy (for example in Bolivia, Ghana, and Viet Nam). The curriculum, a key piece of national legislation, is often amended after changes in government or as a result of the influence of powerful social movements. A national education policy and a national curriculum document express the state's commitment in terms of providing education for all children.

Gender equality and the curriculum

In order to increase demand for girls' education, the value and relevance of the education must be clear. The way in which girls, their families, and teachers view education and the content of the curriculum, will be influenced by gender equality in wider society. Across the world, assumptions about what is appropriate for boys and girls to learn can undermine equality in learning. For example, in many societies it is assumed that girls are not good at mathematics and that boys cannot learn about the care of young children.

Curriculum assumptions such as these, and the teaching that accompanies them, may reinforce gender inequalities, with girls often channelled into 'lower status' subjects. In western Europe and North America, as well as in countries such as Peru, Bangladesh, and South Africa, girls have gained equal *access* to schooling. However this does not mean they have gained equal access to the *curriculum*, and the power that is related to certain types of knowledge.

Box 2.1 A holistic approach to (gender) equality in the curriculum

In textbooks used for Hindi language teaching in Madhya Pradesh, there has been a conscious effort to present girls in positive roles. Famous women from history are included, for example, women who fought for their states, and women renowned for their educational achievements and service to society. Clear messages on the importance of girls' education and the need for equal opportunities are included.

However, the tendency to cast the positive roles of women in the characters of the idealised and exceptionally heroic has not been very effective. In addition, gender stereotyping and inequalities persist in the narratives. Women appear largely in maternal roles, while the decision makers and protectors tend to be male. In one textbook (now revised) a lesson on women's empowerment was placed next to a lesson with a very patronising and alienating description of a tribal community, which was labelled as a criminal community.[1]

The dynamics of teaching and learning in the classroom

Development of the curriculum to address gender inequality cannot happen in isolation from other aspects of schooling, particularly ways of teaching, learning, and interaction within the classroom. Whatever the content of the curriculum, equity will not be achieved if girls are discouraged from speaking, if boys absorb a disproportionate amount of the teachers' energy, nor if the physical environment does not support equal access to education (for example, the provision of girls' toilets and wheelchair access).

Some of the reasons why girls encounter learning problems include the low expectations of teachers regarding their intellectual abilities, coupled with a low level of feedback from teachers. In addition, in some countries teachers say that they enjoy teaching boys more than girls, especially if the girls are seen as passive. Girls' low expectations of themselves contribute to the problem, as does a lack of female teachers in high-status subjects, such as maths and science. Textbooks often reinforce the low expectations of women and girls, as do curriculum and examination materials, while the use of physical space in schools also marginalises girls.[2]

The curriculum is only as good as the teachers who deliver it. Despite extensive gender inequalities outside school, teachers *can* make a difference inside school. If teachers assume that a girl *can* learn mathematics, it will affect their approach to teaching girls and their expectations of what girls can achieve in the subject. If teachers are seen as *facilitators* of learning, rather than merely deliverers of knowledge, then they are *obliged* to ensure that all children learn.

Good policy frameworks on gender equality are a first step in addressing the problem, and many governments have them. A second step is to ensure that these frameworks guide the development of good policies on ways of teaching and learning in order to achieve high-quality results. To improve practice, teachers, head teachers, and government officers need training, and their ways of working need to be endorsed and supported by the community.

What might a gender-equitable approach to schooling look like?

Gender equality can be associated with a superficial focus on girls' education, to the exclusion of boys. There is a need to go beyond simple access issues and ensure a comprehensive understanding of gender. A gender-equity programme should make an assessment of the school looking at four key questions:

- What perceptions of masculinity and femininity are children bringing to school, and what are they acting out in the classroom and the playground?

- What are the dominant images of masculinity and femininity that the school conveys to children?

- Is gender equality a concern in terms of what the school wants and expects of its teachers?

- What initiatives, strategies, and projects, can the whole school undertake to develop a programme for gender equality?[3]

Making schools more 'girl-friendly' and gender-equitable means challenging the culture of authority, hierarchy, and social control in the majority of schools. At a general level (it will differ according to context), it would mean changes to curriculum and to classroom organisation to allow increased participation of girls and women. A 'girl-friendly' school would encourage questioning of the curriculum, the breaking down of hierarchies and power networks that exclude girls and women. Head teachers and teachers would have a greater understanding of the conditions which lead to bullying, racism, sexism, and homophobic behaviour, replacing them with more successful forms of intervention. In addition, some value would be placed on students' experience and knowledge, with students being more actively involved in planning and evaluating their work. Students would be encouraged to challenge narrow-minded concepts, and prejudices, and envision an expanded and divergent future.[4]

Making teaching and the curriculum gender-equitable

There is already a great deal of work being done at national and international levels to influence curriculum change to include gender equality, and to make governments accountable (although this work on accountability tends to focus more closely on issues of quality in general than on gender).

Box 2.2 Partnerships for non-formal curriculum development

Experience in India has shown that developing courses and curricula for out-of-school and adolescent girls calls for strategic and effective partnerships in practice. This would ensure a sharing of expertise between university professionals, women's groups, NGOs, and education functionaries, for the transforming potential of the course to be fully explored.

Curriculum design for non-formal education, through academic–activist partnerships, was put in place in programmes such as Mahila Samakhya, Lok Jumbish, and the National Literacy Campaigns. For instance, curricula and resource manuals on health education were developed for a residential course for young women, and numeracy manuals were prepared using women's indigenous knowledge of folk and street mathematics.[5]

In schools and teacher-training colleges the curriculum is usually full, which means it is not easy to integrate a gender-equality perspective in the design, content, and teaching approach of the many subjects that teachers may have to cope with. Moreover, curricula are often developed by experts and 'owned' by the state, so it is difficult to lobby for change where this might be seen to challenge government control. But, where diversity is recognised and participatory processes are employed, women and girls from different backgrounds can participate in discussions about curriculum decisions and how they are represented – considering that they are a diverse group.

When considering how teaching and the curriculum can be made gender-equitable, these areas need attention:

- *Curriculum content:* we need to consider what girls from poor and marginalised environments are offered by their schooling, and to provide, for example, literacy learning in a way that enhances their confidence, so that they can begin to transform their lives.

- *Learning materials:* often images in textbooks are simply 'check-listed' for their portrayal of gendered images. Children do not necessarily have simplistic, preconditioned responses to images in textbooks, and we need a more sophisticated understanding of, and response to, how children learn about gender from textbooks.

- *Language of instruction and literacy:* children who are geographically or culturally marginalised from mainstream education may find themselves being taught in a language that they do not use. Girls and women often have less access to, and use of, national or 'prestige' languages than men. In what ways is the language of instruction empowering or disabling for girls and boys differently?

- *Methods of evaluation and assessment:* examinations tend to dominate assessment, but other methods should be used, such as continuous assessment. 'Girls could have more equal opportunities in school if teachers talk to them more and encourage them, for instance by giving them prizes for participating in different classroom activities'.[6]

Educating the teachers

Types of gender-training courses

Governments have a responsibility to develop gender equality in teaching through the courses and practical materials that they provide. Teacher education needs to equip teachers to promote an understanding of the profound nature of gender inequity and to overcome the resultant barriers to learning. Ensuring that gender equity is a *central theme* throughout a programme of teacher education, rather than delivered in one-off sessions, is likely to ingrain understanding more effectively. Training needs to help teachers to develop practical solutions, and should be accompanied by monitoring and follow-up support. The efforts of pre-service training institutions, providers of in-service and ongoing professional development, need to be co-ordinated, and well-documented. Building networks of teachers to work together or collaborating through school clusters and teachers' centres, are ways of sustaining training and providing ongoing support for teachers and education officials.[7]

Box 2.3 Training teachers for gender equality, Mukono, Uganda

With the introduction of Universal Primary Education in Uganda in 1997, there was a huge expansion in enrolment, and hundreds of untrained or unlicensed teachers were employed to meet the new demands. The Teacher Development Management Scheme (TDMS) was introduced to promote gender equality in education and convey information about HIV and AIDS. TDMS co-ordinating tutors are used as important mediators between policy makers and teachers, and between policy makers and representatives of the community and parents. They make teachers aware of the gender dynamics of classrooms, and the kinds of identities and relationships that boys and girls forge at school. Teachers are encouraged to see their pupils both as sons and daughters of parents with particular views about education, and as boys and girls with rights and obligations.[8]

Relationships and styles of learning

The teaching process is about the relationships between teachers and learners in schools. What is considered to be 'good' teaching and what promotes successful learning will change, according to who is involved and the context in which the learning takes place. Teachers need to be able to work with different learning styles. Teacher education needs to equip teachers to work through some of the implications of local gender issues, and to support teachers in developing the confidence to encourage participation from pupils and the local community in shaping a vision for gender equality. For example, men tend to dominate school management committees, while women fulfil the more domestic roles. The school needs to interact with the local community to ensure that significant local issues of gender inequality (for example, abuse of girls by their peers and by teachers) are analysed and addressed.

Teaching and living gender equality

Teacher education also needs to address not only how teachers and other education officials *teach* gender equality, but how they *live* this in their private lives, changing personal behaviour and challenging some of the deeply held assumptions that perpetuate inequalities. Student teachers, and in-service teachers, need opportunities to examine and understand their own gender identities, and to understand how gender discrimination takes place in schools, as well as their role in addressing it.[9] For example, teachers have to learn how to make their students aware of their sexuality and, in the age of HIV and AIDS, provide a model of risk-free behaviour.

Linking the school and the community

In tandem with the school, clubs and parents'/students'/teachers' associations can provide venues and forums where strong gender-equality messages can be explored and reinforced. Different types of extra-curricular activities can help children who have been silenced to articulate their needs. There is a need for teachers, NGOs, and community-based organisations to work alongside parents and communities to think about the ways in which they can support boys and girls to learn well at school, in order that both can participate in society.

Box 2.4 Girls' clubs in Liberia

The Forum for African Women Educationalists (FAWE) has promoted girls' clubs in Kenya, Rwanda, Senegal, and Tanzania. In Liberia, together with Oxfam GB, FAWE has introduced after-school clubs for girls in primary and junior-high schools to encourage them to continue with schooling, and to help them analyse their educational problems and find ways of solving them. The girls are mostly living independently in severe economic hardship, and struggling to continue schooling in a social environment characterised by violence and displacement.

Each club receives start-up funding to help the girls to generate further resources for their club through activities such as making and selling soap. FAWE/Oxfam support for the clubs includes training of the club supervisor, gender training for school staff, and workshops for girls on topics such as HIV and AIDS, sexual violence, and family planning.

Future plans to develop the clubs include introducing a life-skills programme and vocational training for girls.[10]

Recommendations

Make curricula and teaching more gender-equitable

The curriculum, and ways of teaching and learning, can reproduce ideas and practices marked by gender inequality. Gender inequalities, and wider social, political, and economic inequalities, can influence the access that girls and boys have to different parts of the curriculum. Teachers' awareness of, and approaches to, gender issues in teaching and learning, are crucial if gender-equitable education is to be achieved. Curriculum content, the relationship between teachers and students, and teacher education, require special attention and policy development if gender-equitable education is to be achieved.

To achieve the recommendations below, adequate resources are needed, including both financial and human resources. Good practice should be documented, shared, and used to influence policy making and changes in practice.

Governments and non-state providers:

- Ensure that curriculum development involves consultation at all levels of society about gender equality, and what decisions mean for women and girls, especially those who may be marginalised because of language or social practice.

- Develop and implement government-agreed standards for quality and equality in education.

- Ensure that there are strong legal measures to outlaw sexual violence and harassment in school, with clear procedures for dealing with abuse, which are widely communicated.

- Ensure that training in gender equality is included in the teacher-education programme, both in pre-service training and in-service college-based or school-based training.

- Develop the capacity and role of the inspectorate and gender units to support gender equality in the classroom.

- Assess the planning and budgeting processes, and ensure that officials at all levels have the capacity to implement them. Put in place any necessary training.

Head teachers and teachers:

- Inform themselves about existing policy for gender equality.

- Develop school-level policies for gender-equitable approaches to teaching and learning.

- Move beyond gender stereotypes and investigate the school's and teachers' own values and culture, and aspirations for gender equality.

- Be trained and empowered to analyse and challenge gender stereotyping and gender bias in curriculum materials, in language use and relations in the school and with the community.

- Recognise the many pressures on women teachers, and encourage supportive networks and practices.

Parents and community members:

- Take an active interest in their children's learning and ensure that the school learning environment is healthy and safe.

- Play an active part in the management of the education resources to ensure they are used for the benefit of both girls and boys equitably.

Notes

1   Adapted from A. Sharma (2003) 'Experiences of Thinking through Gender Equality and the Curriculum: The Case of Madhya Pradesh', Beyond Access Seminar 1, http://k1.ioe.ac.uk/schools/efps/GenderEducDev/Amita%20Sharma%20paper.pdf.

2   Adapted from M. Arnot (2004) 'Gender Equality and Opportunities in the Classroom: Thinking about Citizenship, Pedagogy and the Rights of Children', Beyond Access Seminar 2, http://k1.ioe.ac.uk/schools/efps/GenderEducDev/Arnot%20paper.pdf.

3   Adapted from C. Skelton (2002), in M. Arnot (2004) *ibid.*

4   Adapted from G. Weiner (2004) 'Learning from Feminism: Education, Pedagogy and Practice', Beyond Access Seminar 2, http://k1.ioe.ac.uk/schools/efps/GenderEducDev/Gaby%20Weiner%20paper.pdf.

5   Adapted from A. Sharma (2003) *op.cit.*

6   K. Burns (2004) 'Uganda: Harriet Nambubiru Talks to Kim Burns', in *Equals*, Issue 6.

7   The issue of teacher recruitment is discussed in Chapter 6.

8   E. Unterhalter, E. Kioko Echessa, R. Pattman, R. Rajagopalan, and F. N'Jai (2004) 'Scaling Up Girls' Education: Towards a Scorecard on Girls' Education in the Commonwealth', Beyond Access Project, Institute of Education, University of London and Oxfam GB.

9   F. Chege (2004) 'Teachers' Gendered Lives, HIV/AIDS and Pedagogy', Beyond Access Seminar 2, http://k1.ioe.ac.uk/schools/efps/GenderEducDev/Chege%20paper.pdf.

10 H. Johnston and S. Aikman (2005) 'Discussion Paper on the Liberia Education Programme', Oxford: Oxfam GB.

3. Gender equality and adult basic education

This chapter highlights the fact that the Millennium Development Goals (MDGs) do not directly address the issue of adult basic education and literacy, in spite of these being essential for achieving the Millennium targets. It explores the potential of adult basic education with gender equality to be transformatory for individuals, and for groups working to address key issues, such as gender-based violence, and HIV and AIDS. The role of governments and other key agencies in relation to gender equality and adult basic education is also explored. The chapter concludes with a discussion of how to develop longer-term approaches to gender equality, adult basic education, and literacy.

Adult basic education and the Millennium Development Goals

There are almost 800 million illiterate adults worldwide, of whom 64 per cent are women.[1] There is widespread agreement that adult basic education and literacy enhance human and social development and underpin the achievement of all MDGs. Yet the MDGs do not emphasise or address the eradication of adult illiteracy or the provision of basic education for adults and out-of-school youth. The education Goal (MDG2) focuses on universal primary education. The gender Goal (MDG3) has targets for gender parity in the formal primary, secondary, and tertiary education system, but leaves out adult basic education. There is an urgent need to expand the vision of both these MDGs to take on board basic education for adults.

Literacy and women's empowerment

Societies have become increasingly dependent on the printed word, and non-literate people are among the poorest and least powerful in the world. Marginalised groups and individuals receive little or no education. This particularly affects poor women and girls who experience forms of discrimination and injustice.

There is a close relationship between literacy, power, and empowerment. The objectives of adult basic education and literacy have been expressed by a wide-ranging global consensus 'to enable people and communities to take control of their destiny and society....'.[2]

Box 3.1 National Literacy Programme, Uganda

An evaluation of the National Literacy Programme in Uganda showed that, among positive outcomes, the empowerment or increased self-confidence of learners were perhaps the most salient. One woman expressed this by saying that, before becoming a literacy learner, 'I talked with my hands in front of my mouth without looking up, but now I feel strong and free to speak up.'[3]

There are many providers of literacy teaching, with funding from numerous sources. They use a wide range of approaches, from teaching specific skills and knowledge for limited purposes (e.g. literacy linked to income-generation schemes), through to facilitating learning to achieve more far-reaching empowerment and social change. In other words, adult basic education and literacy teaching does not have to be restricted to teaching people to read and write. While not all literacy learning is empowering in this way, and women sometimes report literacy classes that fall far short of this, it does have the potential to *transform* poor people's lives. This transformation can powerfully challenge gender inequality:

*   Through the teaching process itself, which can promote dialogue, supporting and encouraging learners to discuss and reflect on their condition and its causes.

*   By equipping learners with the skills to gain information and to advocate for their own rights.

Although adult basic education and literacy programmes have the poten
to be empowering for women and girls, a wide-ranging assessment
literacy programmes shows that few have explicitly 'gendered' aims or
gender policies. Of those that do, the aims related to gender range from the
achievement of equal access to programmes, to the transformation of the
lives of women outside the classroom.

Research in a number of settings indicates that, for poor women's lives to be
transformed through gender-equitable adult basic education and literacy
teaching, the content and processes used must be guided by the experiences
and aspirations of the learners, so that they feel relevant to them. Pertinent
and continuing training of teachers to this end is necessary.

Box 3.2 Total Literacy Campaign, India

From the late 1980s, the NGO Bharat Gyan Vigyan Samiti (BGVS) worked in partnership with the Government of India on the Total Literacy Campaign, the aim of which
was to mobilise women for literacy. The campaign, which used messages that linked
literacy to basic livelihood problems, and questions of exploitation and discrimination
against women, provided new hope and optimism for millions of women from all
classes. It gave women a social sanction to come out of their houses and participate
in activities organised in their villages. Today the BGVS is in the process of building
institutional support at the village level for women working with self-help groups.
The objectives of these groups include providing a focus for activities for women's
empowerment, helping women to upgrade their literacy skills and, through micro-
credit enterprises, enhancing their status in the family and in the community.[4]

The realities of women's lives

Illiterate women are a very diverse constituency. What individuals wish to
achieve and change through becoming educated and literate will vary
according to their circumstances and the environments in which they live.
Case studies show that participatory methods for programme design can
ensure that these wishes are a central part of literacy programmes.

Changes in the wider external environment – for example, macro-economic
policy that involves a reduction in government spending on the social sector
because of external debt, or a reduction in the prices paid for crops that
women produce – can directly affect women's lives. Rapid change, such as
that due to a government adopting policies on gender equality or due to

widespread unemployment, can result in confused perceptions of the divisions of work between women and men. This can lead to backlashes against women's independence if, for example, it creates new or different demands for literacy and organised learning.

Increasingly, for many women, living with HIV and AIDS is a reality. Levels of education have been found to be a strong predictor of levels of knowledge about safe behaviour and ways of reducing infection. Education programmes for young people worldwide are addressing HIV prevention with increasing coherence. However, in adult basic education the learning and knowledge is fragmented and dispersed. Adult basic education needs to provide support to learners to help them consider HIV and AIDS from both personal and local perspectives, and women need to be supported to negotiate safe sex.

The vulnerability of women and girls to gender-based violence also makes them more vulnerable to HIV. Women and girls report violence through enforced sex in the domestic sphere, and as a result of conflict and war. These experiences can have profound effects on their confidence and outlook and therefore on their ability to learn. Adult basic education and literacy programmes need to consider how to support their learning, by enabling them to reflect on their experiences.

Box 3.3 HIV and AIDS, gender, and adult basic education in Thailand

The AIDS Education Programme of Chiangmai University has been collaborating with the Asian-South Pacific Bureau of Adult Education (ASPBAE) in developing a set of participatory tools to promote HIV and AIDS awareness and gender aware-ness in the community. The tools are designed to help women and men analyse the linkages between gender (gender inequalities), development (issues of poverty and migration), and HIV and AIDS. They include techniques for analysing gender values and selecting marriage partners; women's work and men's work; risk behaviours and connections among groups in the community; gender roles and values in HIV prevention and care; and gender differences in the control of, and access to, resources in HIV prevention and care.

The research and application of the tools emphasises the need for adult basic education and awareness-raising about HIV and AIDS to be closely linked to other spheres of education, social action, and structural change. It also suggests the need for gender-sensitivity training for young men and women as well as for service providers, community leaders, and faith-based leaders – all gatekeepers to women's equality.[5]

What is needed?

For adult basic education programmes to be gender-equitable and to recognise the local impacts of poverty, discrimination against women, and HIV and AIDS, they need to be closely linked to social action and structural change focusing on poverty alleviation measures, side by side with their engagement with the whole range of education provision.

Support and training for literacy workers in exploring these issues, and links with other support services, need to be established. Training and awareness-raising among trainers, youth leaders, and students of how prevailing gender biases and relationships increase the vulnerability of women, especially to HIV and AIDS, is necessary. In addition, literacy workers need to be able to help both women and men to discuss forms of gender inequality.

If adult basic education is to play a role in transforming the lives of learners, staff need to be trained in participatory practices that include women and men, so that they can support learners by developing locally appropriate materials, available in languages appropriate for a range of learners.

The short-termism that is often in evidence in adult basic education and literacy programmes also needs to be addressed. In many cases, short-term instruction is given (e.g. for six months), without the follow-up needed to consolidate learning and promote reading. This can have a negative impact on women who may be constrained in their mobility to find another class or who have little spare income to buy follow-up materials.

The current lack of training for teachers and facilitators, and the shortage of institutions providing training in empowering methods for the delivery of adult basic education, both need to be addressed. There are few staff-development opportunities or incentives. Volunteers, often women, are poorly remunerated, despite their potential and their commitment.

Box 3.4 The Bolsa Escola Programme in Brazil: empowering mothers and women

The Bolsa Escola programme is best known for its objective of providing families with income subsidies, conditional on keeping their children in school. However, a second objective of the programme, currently being implemented by Oxfam GB and the NGO Missão Criança with EU funding, is to empower women within the family. A mother's level of education, her race, and her level of income, are all factors that correlate strongly with the educational achievement of children in Brazil.

The programme, entitled 'Education to Confront Poverty', provides adult education for mothers and other members of their families, and creates incentives for mothers to participate directly in school meetings and local education councils. The potential for women's participation already exists in some contexts, but there are no real incentives for them to get involved. So, by putting women in charge of receiving and allocating the benefits of the programme, their self-esteem is boosted and their decision-making influence within the family is promoted. Merely putting them in charge of Bolsa Escola funds is not enough: instead, the programme is helping them to become agents of change in their families and communities and to develop skills that can transform their lives.[6]

Neglect of the sector by governments

Governments state that they are committed to adult basic education and literacy – but in reality they are a low priority for most. Adult basic education has remained under-funded and marginalised within ministries, resulting in poor cohesion and co-ordination in adult basic education programmes. Current government neglect of the sector needs to be reversed.

Where they exist, large-scale government-funded adult basic education and literacy programmes are usually weakened by short-termism – they are one-offs with no budget or plan for follow-up. Adult education has been addressed through patchy and unco-ordinated programmes and work by NGOs and community-based organisations. These often rely on short-term funding.

This is not a promising backdrop for the development of more sophisticated gender-equitable policies and practices. In order to deliver gender-equitable adult basic education and literacy programmes, governments need to ensure that, rather than being rigid and prescriptive, programmes are sensitive to variations in context, respectful of differences, innovative, and responsive to a range of challenges for building gender equality. Literacy programmes must operate at a local level. Decentralised support services appear to be the most successful means of enabling this, but these need adequate resourcing. Where it exists, good practice should be documented and shared.

Governments must be held accountable for the commitments they have articulated. A policy framework for adult basic education and literacy, based on democratic rights, is needed in most countries to clarify the commitment and role of the state. Where this exists on paper, there needs to be a push to ensure delivery and support stronger forums and networks among the range of education providers, for gender equality.

The role of civil society

The key challenge for civil society is to lobby governments through advocacy, campaigning, and provision for an overall gender-equity approach to *all* education, by linking the focus on girls' formal education contained in the Millennium Development Goals to adult basic education and literacy for women.

NGOs need to highlight for governments the potential of participatory approaches in adult basic education and literacy to achieve gender equality and social change. While willing to promote literacy through partnerships with NGOs, governments may become unsupportive or even hostile when mobilisation for literacy leads to a wider social mobilisation of women advocating for their rights.

Movements need to advocate for governments to establish a rights-based policy framework, and governments need to ensure that a process exists to achieve this. This means building dialogue with governments.

There is a huge role for civil society to play in raising the profile of adult basic education and literacy and ensuring that it is gender-equitable. NGOs have developed collaborations, such as the Global Campaign for Education, to advocate for governments to honour commitments they have made. More resources are needed to strengthen advocacy for change to public policies, so that these confront gender exclusion in the lack of education for adults and promote education with gender justice.

Adult basic education and literacy are important in themselves, and also for key areas such as health, leadership, and the broad issues of women's empowerment. Through greater advocacy, adult basic education needs to be moved higher up the agenda of the women's movement and higher among the concerns of civil society.

Box 3.5 Advocacy for gender justice in education

In 1990 the Women's Popular Education Network (REPEM) launched a campaign in Latin America to change the image of women in education programmes and in the media. With little financial support or political will and in a context of sexism at all levels of education, the campaign worked to influence:

- the availability of adult basic education;

- UN summits and conferences, particularly the Fifth International Conference on Adult Education (CONFINTEA V);

- social movements (e.g. the World Social Forum) and women's movements where education was not a priority.

Since then, REPEM has developed into a strong network able to participate in the preparatory process of each UN conference at local, regional, and global levels. It prepares documents, reviews ongoing activities, and monitors the implementation of agreements made by governments and by previous conferences. The campaign fights not only for the physical inclusion of women in adult basic education, but also to overcome the exclusion of women based on other areas of difference: age, social class, race, ethnicity, or sexual orientation.[7]

Recommendations

Governments:

- Develop a policy framework for adult basic education and literacy that is part of an integrated education policy;

- Work closely with civil-society organisations to design and develop this framework and subsequent policies;

- Prioritise financial and human resources to support the implementation of good-quality adult basic education and literacy that transforms gender relations;

- Form relationships and programmes with donors who prioritise adult basic education (e.g. SIDA, the Swedish International Development Cooperation Agency); and

- Develop human resources and capacity, together with adequate funding, at local levels of government (i.e. training, curriculum development, research, and documentation).

Civil-society actors:

- Lobby for investment in adult basic education as a necessity for achieving all the MDGs;

- Lobby governments and funding agencies to develop strategies to achieve commitments related to adult basic education in the Dakar Framework of Action for Education for All;

- Lobby to achieve the Beijing Platform for Action;

- Develop strong links with women's movements and organisations campaigning on HIV and AIDS and aspects of poverty.

Adult educators and civil-society organisations together need to develop transformative gender practices by broadening the concept of literacy, from simply learning to read and write, to learning and developing skills for social action and women's empowerment. They need to campaign for more creative and participatory training of trainers, with action research linked to local gender needs and the diversity of learners, and to document good practice to improve understanding of how literacy is developed in different social contexts and actions.

Notes

1 UNESCO (2005) 'Education for All – Literacy for Life', EFA Global Monitoring Report 2006', Paris: UNESCO.

2 Fifth International Conference on Adult Education (CONFINTEA V), Declaration 5, http://www.unesco.org/education/uie/confintea/documents.html.

3 A. Lind (2004) 'Reflections on Gender Equality and National Adult Basic Education', Beyond Access Seminar 4, available at: http://ioewebserver.ioe.ac.uk/ioe/cms/get.asp?cid=7746&7746_0=10874, last accessed March 2007.

4 K. Srivastava (2004) 'Community Mobilisation, Gender Equality, and Resource Mobilisation in Adult Basic Education', Beyond Access Seminar 4, available at: http://ioewebserver.ioe.ac.uk/ioe/cms/get.asp?cid=7746&7746_0=10874, last accessed March 2007.

5   U. Duongsaa (2004) 'Development, Gender, HIV/AIDS, and Adult Education', Beyond Access Seminar 4, available at:
http://ioewebserver.ioe.ac.uk/ioe/cms/get.asp?cid=7746&7746_0=10874, last accessed March 2007.

6   L. Palazzo (2005) 'Bolsa Escola, Brazil: Enabling Enrolment and Empowerment', *Equals* newsletter 11.

7   C. Eccher (2004) 'Gender and Education: History of Some Struggles', Beyond Access Seminar 4, available at: http://ioewebserver.ioe.ac.uk/ioe/cms/get.asp?cid=7746&7746_0=10874, last accessed March 2007.

4. Beyond the mainstream

Education for nomadic and pastoralist girls and boys

This chapter illustrates the challenges involved in providing good-quality gender-equitable education for children who are beyond the reach of mainstream, formal education. It focuses on children of nomadic and pastoralist households, identifying specific issues in providing schooling for them, and drawing on lessons from approaches and initiatives by various agencies (government and non-government). The chapter explores specific forms of discrimination that nomadic and pastoralist girls experience in relation to education, and highlights the need for deeper gender analysis in order to inform policy making.

Nomadic and pastoralist children beyond the mainstream

It is estimated that there are between 25 million and 40 million children of school age living in nomadic or pastoralist households of whom only between 10 per cent and 50 per cent attend school. Between 15 million and 25 million of the estimated 100 million of out-of-school children are probably nomads and pastoralists.[1] While rates of participation and completion of basic education for pastoralist boys are very low, the rates for girls are far lower.

This chapter draws primarily on evidence from NGO programme reports and research across West, Central, and East Africa with mobile and semi-mobile livestock herders. In these regions many pastoralist and nomadic societies are characterised by poverty and particular aspects of gender inequalities, such as a rigid division of labour coupled with a heavy workload for all members of households. Other distinguishing features of these societies include the harsh effects of desertification and chronic drought, the way that migration by men often entails further work for women, the practice of early marriage, and in some cases a belief in the intellectual inferiority of women and girls. While policies and practices need to address issues particular to pastoralists and nomads in general, they also need to address issues specific to pastoralist and nomadic women and girls.

Nomadic and pastoralist children still do not enjoy their right to a basic education.[2] The 2015 Education for All target will not be achieved unless policies and resources are directed to provide these children with access to relevant, good-quality education. There is little evidence, however, that pastoralist education has been addressed through major national initiatives in any country, with the exceptions of Uganda and Mongolia,[3] since the World Education Forum in 1990.

Box 4.1 Enrolment of pastoralist girls and boys in Kenya

With the declaration of Free Primary Education (FPE) in Kenya in 2003, a national Gross Enrolment Rate of 104 per cent was achieved. Despite this overall increase, the figures obscured geographical inequalities and, in pastoralist districts, the Gross Enrolment Rate was only 25 per cent, with as few as 17 per cent of pastoralist girls enrolled in school. This suggests that fees were not the only obstacle to enrolment. Hidden costs, such as uniforms, lunch, and community-development funds, as well as unfriendly school environments lacking adequate sanitation facilities, have further excluded girls, rather than boys. Low rates of participation are also strongly influenced by mobility of pastoralist families.

Wajir Girls' Primary School in the north-east of Kenya was founded in 1988 following a road accident: a bus crashed while ferrying pastoralist girls from Wajir to a boarding school 200 kilometres away in Garissa, killing the girls on board. The community raised its own funds to construct a girls-only primary school. Enrolment has since risen from 40 girls to 576 girls, and the school has now been incorporated into the government system. The school's popularity reflects a community activism on behalf of girls' education, often by those who have been educated themselves, in a district where there is also very strong opposition to educating girls. Female teachers have been trained to promote gender equality and do this through, among other things, running workshops exploring issues such as girls' rights and cultural practices, including female genital mutilation.[4]

In terms of education, the *mobility* of nomads and pastoralists is a significant issue. This can be daily mobility, such as the movements of the Eritrean sheepherders, or more extensive travelling, such as the seasonal journeys of Touareg sheep and camel herders. As a result of their mobility, pastoralist and nomadic children are unable to attend a static school during the usual daytime hours of a conventional school year. Children in travelling families, who do not see themselves as nomads or pastoralists, are in a similar position.

Box 4.2 Gender relations among nomadic and semi-nomadic pastoralists in Uganda

Participatory Rural Appraisal (PRA) studies carried out by the Alternative Basic Education for Karamoja (ABEK) programme working with pastoralist groups in Uganda, show that women are the main producers in pastoral society, accounting for 90 per cent of domestic labour. They make a significant contribution to livestock production but do not own livestock or land, have the highest illiteracy rate, have limited access to credit and modern technology, and suffer from domestic violence. Early marriages have denied many girls the chance to realise their potential, and men dominate decision making at household and community levels. Women's power to make decisions is mainly in the choice of crops to be planted, and even then men initiate decisions and only really present conclusions to their wives for approval.[5]

What nomads and pastoralists want from formal education

Nomad and pastoralist girls and boys have a right to good-quality basic education, but nomadic and pastoralist girls access less education than boys, and their participation and achievements are much lower than those of boys. In order to design a flexible education policy and deliver gender-equitable education, policy makers need to identify what motivates nomads and pastoralists to send their children to school, understand the expectations and motivations of girls and their households, and then develop strategies that take account of their expectations. There is a lack of relevant data about nomads and pastoralists in general, and women and girls in particular.

Evidence from fieldwork suggests that nomadic and pastoralist families' own informal education of their children is concerned with teaching them about their way of life and their values. Few adults have themselves had the opportunity to go to school, and where there are opportunities they may send only some children to school, usually the boys. There is also evidence that nomadic and pastoralist households see schooling as part of an overall strategy based on their assessment of employment prospects, different sources of income, and vulnerability. When environmental change, conflict, or other factors put severe pressure on their ways of life, they look to formal education to provide alternatives for their children, especially their sons. For some, formal education is seen as a way to an alternative means of livelihood from pastoralism.

When pastoralist and nomadic parents send their children to school, they do not want a substandard education, but one which is both the same as others receive, with the same certification, and is also relevant to their mobility, way of life, and knowledge.

Box 4.3 The Ngorongoro Early Childhood Development programme, Tanzania

The community-based Early Childhood Development (ECD) programme in Ngorongoro province has established ECD centres next to bomas (Maasai home-steads) in order to make sure that they are accessible to both boys and girls. Each centre has two Maasai teachers – one male and one female – who are trained in active-learning techniques, which encourage them to involve all children equally. These local teachers are sensitive to the cultural background of the children and they are trained in a gender-sensitive way. The ECD centres are run by management and both men and women are involved in decision making on issues affecting the centre.[6]

Specific policy issues

Decentralisation and financing

Basic education should be free for all boys and girls at the point of delivery. Governments should make specific allocations to ensure adequate financing for pastoralist education, but in reality the opposite is what happens. Although pastoralist and nomadic peoples contribute substantially to the overall national economy and to government revenues through, for example, taxes on their livestock, they do not benefit from investment in their education. For example, in harsh climatic conditions, with a low-population density and poor communications and infrastructure, basic services (including health facilities and schools) are to be found only in towns. Children whose families are mobile or semi-mobile cannot attend these schools on a regular basis. Mobile schools, where teachers with a minimum of materials move with the students, have been tried in several countries with different degrees of success, but today they are considered to be too costly by local education authorities in poor areas, which have no means of raising local revenue for schooling. Moreover, mobile schooling is not often a priority for local or national governments with explicit or implicit policies of sedentarisation for mobile peoples. Boarding schools have also been established in towns to cater for children from mobile families, but these have often been hampered by lack of demand, high running costs, poor facilities, shortages of regular supplies of food, and lack of security, particularly for girls.

Government decentralisation and civil-society participation are often considered to be essential for successful development. However, decentralisation, combined with economic liberalisation and privatisation of the education system, cannot automatically be considered beneficial. For example, when central government devolves the financing of education to district level in nomadic pastoralist zones, the ability of local government to raise revenue for schooling through taxation is often very weak. The result is that communities have to bear a heavy financial responsibility to ensure that schools function, and where schools *are* accessible, girls will be the losers if parents cannot afford to send all their children to school. As nomadic and pastoralist peoples generally live in the poorest parts of a country, they feel the financial burden of providing education services more than other wealthier communities. It is important to understand the implications for both girls and boys of budget decisions and policy making, at both national and decentralised levels of government.

Charges for basic education, both user fees and hidden expenses, are especially unreasonable for nomadic and pastoral peoples. The financial burden is too great for parents to cover their children's expenses in boarding schools. When pastoralists *have* managed to contribute financially to their children's education, the opportunity costs are high. For example, pastoralism is labour-intensive, and children's contribution to the work is important. It is girls who walk great distances to fetch water for domestic use, and who also play a major role in watering the animals; this makes their labour an important contribution to the household economy. It is also the girls who have to fetch water for the school.

What kinds of school for gender equality?

Decisions about where to locate static schools have important implications for girls. Pastoralist children living in dispersed mobile groups may have many kilometres to walk each day to and from school. This raises safety issues for girls en route, and also in school, where they may be far from their family and therefore more vulnerable to abuse. In drought-stricken pastoralist zones of the Sahel, in-school feeding programmes are essential if boys and girls are to attend school, given the many hours they spend walking there and back. Parents may let their sons sleep on the school floor during the week, but not their daughters. If schools have no toilets or running water that is safely accessible to girls, they may miss many weeks a year of schooling while they are menstruating. Flexibility in the timing of the school day and annual calendar of the school is very important in relation to workloads, and these all need to be examined for their different impact on girls and boys. Creative approaches need to be found, such as developing a network of host families to provide accommodation and security for girls and boys attending school far from home.

Box 4.4 Mobile schools in Darfur, Sudan

The Darfur mobile school is a one-teacher multigrade school, supported by Oxfam GB, set up to provide schooling for small numbers of children travelling with their families in small groups. Low population density, high mobility, and limited demand for schooling mean that, under certain circumstances, a multigrade model can be highly appropriate.

However, the multigrade model approved by the government restricts schooling to only the first four years of basic education. As complete primary schools (i.e. schools offering all six primary grades) are available only in permanent settlements, few nomadic children continue their education for more than four years. This is especially the case for the girls, who are less likely than boys to go on to boarding school or to a static school in a settlement. This raises the question of what results can be achieved in these first four years, and to what extent girls have acquired sustainable skills and developed the expertise that they need for their futures.[7]

Breaking through the barriers to girls' schooling

Government agencies must develop a gender analysis of the obstacles and inequalities faced by nomadic and pastoralist girls and women, both inside and outside of the school. Although providing more schools may increase the *overall* numbers of children who have access to education, this does not necessarily address the lack of opportunities for girls, and it does not confront the problem of how to support girls to remain in school until they have achieved a good-quality education which can improve their capabilities. Depending on the context, successful initiatives to include girls, and to support them to remain in school and complete a basic education, might include girl-only schools, boarding facilities, or female 'animators' working in the community.

Box 4.5 'Animatrices' in Mali and Niger

In pastoralist communities in north-eastern Mali and western Niger, Oxfam GB is working with school and community animatrices, or 'female mobilisers', in order to encourage higher rates of attendance and participation by pastoralist girls in formal schooling. Girls' participation is hindered by a range of issues, including early marriage, their excessive workloads, popular beliefs that women are inferior to men and less intellectually able, and widespread poverty. The animatrices help to tackle some of these issues by working with parents and teachers (mostly male) to change negative attitudes towards girls and schooling, and to reinforce the right to an education. By working in the school and with the teachers, they have helped to make the school environment more friendly to girls, and the walk to school safer.

By linking closely with parents and mobile households, the animatrices have helped fathers and mothers to understand the benefits of schooling for their daughters. As relatively well-educated local women in paid employment, the animatrices serve as positive examples for local girls. They have also encouraged the participation of women in parents' associations and women's groups, where women from otherwise scattered households welcome the opportunity to come together to exchange views and to learn basic literacy.[8]

Teacher policy and curriculum reform

The mobility of nomads and pastoralists means that they are likely to be particularly affected by poor retention of teachers in rural areas. Owing to the generally low education levels among pastoralists, it is difficult to recruit pastoralist teachers for mobile schools. And there are even fewer pastoralist or nomadic women with the appropriate formal qualifications, which means that there are few examples of pastoralist and nomadic women in different and challenging roles. Gender equality is therefore an important issue in the recruitment and retention of teachers. Teachers from outside, who *do* have appropriate education qualifications (though this rarely includes the local language), need strong incentives to work in mobile schools.

To be successful, mobile schools need to challenge well-established ideas of what a school is; mobility may necessitate a shortened school day, involve multigrade teaching (sometimes including adults too), require a truncated school year, and need an adapted curriculum which requires specific relevant training for teachers. In all schools in pastoralist areas, payment of teachers' salaries can be a problem if the government does not have a flexible payment scheme, or has devolved responsibility for payment to local government offices without an adequate budget, or if the community must carry the burden.

Box 4.6 Basic education in the Jijiga and Fik Zones, Somali State, Ethiopia

In the pastoralist areas of Fik and Jijiga in Ethiopia, formal basic education provision reaches only 16 per cent of children, the majority from urban areas. In order to address the severe problem of lack of basic education in rural areas, Save the Children UK, working with the Regional Education Bureau, is implementing an alternative basic education programme for pastoral and agro-pastoral children. An appropriate and relevant curriculum has been developed, adapted from the existing formal education curriculum, and locally recruited teachers are given training in basic teaching skills and subject matter.

The school calendar is flexible, based on the seasonal movement of the community, and the school timetable has been negotiated in order to allow both boys and girls to attend classes. Links with the formal education system have been established in order to allow children who complete the three-year alternative basic education cycle to join the second cycle of primary education in the formal system.[9]

Increasingly, education reforms are providing the framework for governments to develop a national 'core' curriculum with flexibility for local and regional diversity: geographical, social, and cultural. However, local-government officials and teachers do not have the training and skills to adapt the 'core' curriculum to suit their local contexts. In other instances, curriculum modules intended to be relevant to local people are not developed locally at all, but by 'experts' or teachers. National teacher-training curricula need to equip teachers with the skills to be able to make the curriculum locally relevant (for example to respond to the local context of HIV and AIDS), to provide training in teaching the national languages as a second language, and to offer bilingual education. The teaching and learning should build on participatory methods and active learning approaches, and the curriculum should be sensitive to the needs of both girls and boys, responding to social and cultural diversity, both locally and nationally, avoiding general presumptions, and promoting gender equality.

Recommendations

Mere *expansion* of formal education provision, based on a model of what works in urban situations, is not enough to ensure that Education For All reaches nomadic and pastoralist children. Limited provision of static schooling, or projects which have focused on getting nomadic boys and girls to adapt to the formal system, have failed. Experience in the non-formal sector indicates that interventions that are community-based, and that respond to context and mobility patterns, can work. Appropriate modifications, such as adjusting the school calendar to ensure appropriate timing, or adapting the curriculum to ensure its relevance, are necessary. Pastoralist schooling needs to take account of the different work practices of women and men when planning flexible provision of adequate and sustainable resources – both financial and human. It also needs to be sensitive to issues of safe and accessible water supplies and food security, which have a huge impact on schooling opportunities for children in pastoralist zones. It is only when governments have made efforts to reach nomads and pastoralists in innovative ways that completion rates have improved.

NGO methods, and work in collaboration with nomadic and pastoralist communities, indicate that most success in changing ideas and beliefs about education for girls, and increased enrolment and retention, comes when education is not considered in isolation from other social factors.

Policy frameworks

Coherent policy frameworks are needed to accommodate different provisions, and to support a variety of responses to the situations and education needs of nomads and pastoralists, paying particular attention to the interactions between women and men in their societies. However, education for nomadic and pastoralist children must be accorded the same official recognition and status as formal government schooling elsewhere to avoid their further marginalisation. Education must also be attractive to and valued by the nomadic and pastoralist communities. Owing in part to a lack of national cultural, economic, and social data, government or donor education policy rarely refers to the specific situation of nomads and pastoralists, and literature addressing the specific needs of girls and women is very scarce. Therefore nomads and pastoralists are 'invisible' in many national statistics and reports – nomadic and pastoralist women and girls are doubly invisible.

NGOs are active in providing alternative education programmes, often working with local governments, many of which take a multi-activity approach which supports good-quality formal education in the context of community development, women's self-development and organisation, and capacity building on health issues. Examples of good practice need to be documented so that governments can incorporate them into their planning and policy design as part of their official systems.

Specific recommendations for government agencies and non-government agencies include:

Government agencies:

- Base policy on an analysis of the obstacles and inequalities faced by nomadic and pastoralist girls and women, inside and outside school.

- Ensure availability of national-level cultural, economic, and social data on nomads and pastoralists, disaggregated by sex and by region/ province/district, to inform education policy making.

- End user fees and hidden costs for education.

- Provide specific training for teachers to address linguistic and cultural differences and gender inequality, and concurrently promote the training of local teachers.

- Promote participation of nomads and pastoralists in education planning and decision making, and develop policy frameworks in close collaboration with pastoralists and their organisations, including an equal proportion of women in decision making.

- Integrate successful, innovative approaches to pastoralist education into government policy.

Non-government agencies:

- Exchange experiences, communicate, and learn from good practice in order to influence policy and practice. Prioritise gender analysis in all work.

- Raise the profile of nomadic and pastoralist communities' education and specific needs within NGO coalitions.

- Lobby governments and donor agencies for adequate and sustainable financing.

- Encourage community participation in schooling, involving women and men.

- Lobby and work with governments for successful and innovative approaches to pastoralist education that take account of gender equality, so that these can be incorporated into education policy.

Notes

1   Oxfam GB (2003) 'Achieving EFA through Responsive Education Policy and Practice for Nomadic and Pastoralist Children: What can Agencies do?', unpublished paper, Oxford: Oxfam GB.

2   There is considerable debate about whether children of specifically nomadic and pastoralist households are different from other rural or marginalised households because of their mobility, but what is clear is that they suffer multiple discrimination, and there is a need for flexible education policies for millions of children who are beyond the mainstream.

3   Some recent developments at provincial and district levels have taken place in Kenya, Ethiopia, and Sudan.

4   See Oxfam (2005) 'Pastoralist Education Learning Resource: A compilation of information on pastoralist education programmes in Horn and East Africa', Nairobi: Oxfam GB; I. Leggett (2005) 'Learning to improve policy for pastoralists in Kenya', in S. Aikman and E. Unterhalter (eds.), *Beyond Access: Transforming Policy and Practice for Gender Equality in Education*, Oxford: Oxfam GB; and E. Unterhalter, E. Kioko-Echessa, R. Pattman, R. Rajagopalan, and N. Fatmatta (2005) 'Scaling up girls' education: Towards a scorecard on girls' education in the Commonwealth', London: Beyond Access Project. http://ioewebserver.ioe.ac.uk/ioe/cms/get.asp?cid=7746.

5   Oxfam (2005), *op. cit.*, p 65.

6   E. Lugano (2005) Correspondence with author.

7   S. Aikman and H. El Haq (2006) 'EFA for pastoralists in North Sudan: a Mobile Multigrade model of Schooling', in A. Little (ed.) (2006) *Education For All and Multigrade Teaching: challenges and opportunities*, Amsterdam: Springer. The research for this publication and the case study was carried out in 2002. However, due to the current political situation in Darfur, the Oxfam GB programme supporting the mobile schools in Darfur is currently suspended.

8   S. Sanou and S. Aikman (2005) 'Pastoralist Schools in Mali: Gendered Roles and Curriculum Realities', in S. Aikman and E. Unterhalter, *op.cit.*

9   Oxfam (2005), *op. cit.*, p 9.

5. Making it happen

Political will for gender equality in education

Why do some countries succeed in promoting gender parity and equality in education while others do not? The answer often given is 'political will'. All too often, however, no further explanation is offered. There has been little effort to understand why governments are unwilling or unable to change their policies and priorities to achieve equal access to education for girls and boys, as expressed in the third Millennium Development Goal(MDG). This chapter considers the concept of political will and explores the role that it plays in improving gender parity and equality in education.

Commitment, leadership, and responsiveness

Broadly conceived, 'political will' is the sustained commitment of politicians and administrators to invest the necessary resources to achieve specific objectives. It is the *willingness* of these actors to undertake reform and implement policy, despite opposition. Conversely, lack of political will is the absence of such commitment and willingness.[1]

Political will can be further understood in terms of three inter-related concepts: commitment, leadership, and responsiveness.

Commitment

Visible and sustained commitment by elected leaders and administrators is crucial if positive changes in attitudes, policies, and programmes affecting gender equality in education are to take place, and if these changes are to be sustained. Commitment to achieving gender equality and the empowerment of women through equal access to all levels of education by 2015, as expressed in the third MDG, may be *legal* or *political*.

The majority of countries are legally committed to achieving gender equality and universal access to education. This commitment is expressed through the ratification of international conventions, including the Convention on the Elimination of All Forms of Discrimination against Women (CEDAW) and the Convention on the Rights of the Child (CRC). It is also reflected in domestic legislation that guarantees free and compulsory education, and binds a government to meeting national targets for achieving parity of opportunity for girls and boys. Legislation against the abuse of girls is a measure of legal commitment to achieving gender parity in schools: psychological abuse, corporal punishment, sexual harassment, and rape all severely limit the enrolment and retention of female teachers and students in school.

Implementation and enforcement of legal commitments, however, is often weak, and well-intentioned policy becomes diluted or even evaporates as a result. Bangladesh, for instance, has a legal commitment to the provision of free and compulsory education, and has made significant strides towards gender parity. Yet almost half of Bangladeshi households have to make 'donations' to ensure the enrolment of their children. In practice, legal commitment is never enough to ensure girls' access to education. Legal commitment must be supported by political commitment: the commitment by authorities to ensure that legislation and codes of conduct are properly implemented and enforced.

Box 5.1 The gap between policy and practice in Malawi

The government of Malawi changed its policy to permit young mothers to re-enter school after giving birth. Implementation of the policy, however, has been problematic. It has met with resistance from school personnel who were concerned that it would encourage promiscuity, and that young mothers would be a bad influence on other girls in school.[2]

Securing such sustained commitment is difficult, especially when the changes required are contrary to socio-cultural norms and practices. Unsurprisingly, those countries that have been most successful in making rapid progress towards gender parity and equality have been those in which there is a strong and broadly supported ideology of social inclusion. This has been the case in several countries emerging from socio-political upheavals, such as post-revolution Mozambique and post-genocide Rwanda. The experience of these countries suggests that where a process of more general transformation is underway, coinciding with a drive for equality, policy makers have an opportunity to accelerate progress towards gender equality in education. Under such conditions, there is likely to be greater opportunity for introducing radical policy change and implementing institutional reforms which might otherwise run counter to traditional practices – including practices that reflect negative attitudes to girls and women.

Box 5.2 Policies that make a difference for Ugandan girls

In Uganda, the resolve of the Ministry of Education to address the abuse of girls in school has led to the dismissal and imprisonment of some teachers and male students who have had sex with under-age girls. When communities are aware of successful legal cases, and the media draw attention to the issues, other girls are encouraged to speak out. This in turn has the potential to reduce sexual misconduct and violence in schools.[3]

Leadership

The leadership of individuals can create and sustain commitment to the empowerment of girls and women, although 'leadership' is difficult to define. It includes, for example, intelligence and vision, attractive personal qualities, rhetorical and organisational skills, openness to innovation, and a willingness to take risks, make hard choices and set priorities. Leadership is required from a range of actors at central and local levels. At the top, presidents and prime ministers, cabinet members, members of parliament, and ministry officials must exercise leadership to establish and maintain gender equality as a national priority, to ensure that programmes and policies are followed through, and to counter opposition and inertia. Leadership within national-level civil society is also essential if demand for change is to be sustained. At the grassroots level, the leadership of local administrators, head teachers, community organisers, and traditional authorities can drive progress towards gender equality.

Central leadership is crucial. Heads of state have unmatched authority to inspire diverse social and political groups to organise themselves to work for gender equality. The heads of government in China, Morocco, Oman, Sri Lanka, and Uganda have all spoken out in support of girls' education and made it a visible political priority. In Uganda, the state's support for free primary education, and its commitment to girls' education in particular, have contributed to the increased enrolment of both boys and girls in primary school.

Women in positions of authority can exert a particularly important influence on efforts to promote girls' education: they not only act as a role model, but also are in a position to change the priorities and practices of government.[4] The Forum for African Women Educationalists (FAWE) demonstrates that female leaders can be strong advocates for gender equality.

Box 5.3 The Forum for African Women Educationalists (FAWE)

FAWE is an organisational network 'capturing the synergy of ideas, the influence and the power of women leaders working to promote the best interests of girls' education'. Established in 1992, FAWE works both across the African continent and through national chapters. Its programmes include advocacy, policy influencing, and capacity building. Full membership of FAWE includes 32 women ministers and deputy ministers of education, women permanent secretaries in education ministries, women directors of education, and other prominent women educationalists. There are also associate female members (including former full members) and associate male members who are ministers of education committed to FAWE's mandate. The overall success of FAWE can be gauged by the demands of male leaders requesting to be associated with it.[5]

Female leadership, however, is hampered by the fact that there are so few women in positions of authority. Women, for instance, hold fewer than 10 per cent of parliamentary seats in almost all the countries that are struggling to achieve MDG 3. Moreover, with the exception of FAWE, women are often not sufficiently organised to represent powerful pressure groups within governments.

Well-placed individuals with a commitment to gender equality in education can act as champions for girls' education. In Ethiopia, the post of Minister of Education has been filled by one woman since 1992. She has consistently drawn the attention of politicians and policy makers to girls' education. However, depending on the leadership of a few politicians or administrators may not be a reliable way to promote gender parity and equality. Key officials are often transferred from post to post, and elected leaders can be voted out of office. In Guinea, for instance, problems encountered in sustaining a strong gender focal point in the Ministry of Education can be partly attributed to the fact that the Minister (a former member of the FAWE Executive Committee) was moved from her post.

Traditional and religious leaders can play an important role in promoting girls' education, at both national and local levels. In many contexts, marginalising these leaders from efforts to promote gender equality may obstruct progress or create a strong negative reaction. However, where they are involved in the process, traditional and religious leaders are often crucial advocates for reform. In Guinea and Mauritania, religious leaders were called upon to help to create public awareness of the importance of educating girls. The success of this strategy showed that gaining the trust and support of prominent community members ought to be the starting point for any initiative to change negative attitudes towards girls' schooling.[6]

Responsiveness

A third facet of political will is responsiveness. To achieve gender equality, decision makers and education providers must be responsive to the needs, rights, and ambitions of women and girls; to the organisations and individuals acting as their advocates; and to the evidence that demonstrates the value and benefits of gender equality.

Ultimately, political responsiveness entails relationships of **accountability** between citizens (especially women and girls), their government, and education providers. In some cases, as highlighted above, leaders already are responsive and act as champions for girls' education. In many cases, however, such positive developments will not take place unless demand for progress is both loud enough and articulate enough to require a response from decision makers and service providers. Advocates of gender parity and equality must therefore have a way to influence and call to account politicians and other leaders, administrators, and educators.

The recent prominence of school fees as election issues in Malawi, Uganda, Tanzania, and Kenya shows that education can win votes. This is a promising development. However, the likelihood of elections being won or lost on the basis of gender parity and equality in education remains remote.

Civil-society organisations and social movements can use another, less direct, mechanism for amplifying demands for change and holding officials and service providers to account. Where civil society is a strong and vociferous advocate for gender equality, it is more likely that the empowerment of women will remain at the top of the political agenda. Much of the progress made towards increased girls' enrolment in Bangladesh and parts of India and Sri Lanka in the 1990s can be attributed to the combination of a receptive national government and effective campaigning and advocacy by civil-society organisations. These constituencies for change are often spearheaded by educated urban elites which have a strong commitment to education for the masses for instrumental reasons (i.e. to transform poor people's behaviour and attitudes in ways which are likely to have broader benefits). These organisations, therefore, may or may not give 'voice' to poor women in rural areas.

It is often suggested that accountability and responsiveness can be enhanced through **decentralisation** and **community participation**. School management committees (SMCs) and parent–teacher associations (PTAs) in particular have been promoted as mechanisms to strengthen local accountability, although ensuring women's representation on these bodies is often fraught with difficulty. The extent to which SMCs and PTAs are active and operate in the interests of girls' education varies. Evidence suggests that parents themselves often favour boys' education over that of girls where choices have to be made, because the economic returns are perceived to be higher. In such cases, there is no reason to believe that parents, SMCs, PTAs, or communities more generally will prioritise girls' education without strong advocates within the community.

Non-state providers (including the private sector, NGOs, and faith-based organisations) often share the responsibility for meeting the gender parity and equality targets set by national governments. These providers may or may not be committed to the government's agenda. It is often suggested that accountability is stronger where non-state providers are delivering education, because they have to be responsive to their clients. However, this is not the only, or most appropriate, route to ensuring accountability. Encouraging community participation within government schools is another possible route. Even where non-state provision does improve accountability, this may not result in support for gender equality where the clients themselves have preferences for educating sons.

There are some examples of successful collaboration between non-state providers and communities to ensure improvements in girls' education. A good example is that of the Bangladesh Rural Advancement Committee (BRAC). BRAC has pioneered the development of village schools which are managed by parents and teachers who are recruited from the local community, offering a curriculum and timetable that are relevant to local needs, and an education which qualifies children to enter the formal system on graduation.

Box 5.4 Replication of the BRAC model in Malawi

Experience of attempts to replicate the BRAC model in Malawi, where the international NGO (Save the Children-US) established the programme, has shown that once the INGO began its planned withdrawal, community support was not sustained. This was in part because of the demands placed on poor communities, but was also because the INGO had not fostered the development of local NGOs to take over the programme, as intended. As a result, the encouragement of community participation as a means of ensuring local demand and accountability was not maintained.

In addition, the programme did not pay sufficient attention to building national commitment to its work, through identifying a champion within the Ministry of Education, for example. So the Ministry of Education did not take over responsibility for the programme as the plan had envisaged. This highlights the importance of paying attention to the local and national contexts when designing such programmes.[7]

Private providers operating for profit range from those supplying better-quality services to those who can afford it, to ones offering 'last-chance' opportunities where insufficient school places are available. The implications for gender equality vary according to the context. In Nepal, parents overwhelmingly prefer to send their sons to better-quality private schools, while girls are sent off to stay with relatives to attend a government-run school. If the policies and practice of non-state providers are insensitive to the needs of girls, the government may bring them to account through regulation. However, non-state provision of education is most evident in developing countries where the government itself is failing to provide. In such cases, government capacity is too weak to regulate the non-state sector, even if regulation were to include gender-specific concerns.

Development partners

In many countries the strongest advocates of gender equality have been donors, rather than domestic stakeholders. This external pressure for commitments to gender equality has helped to put girls' education on the political agenda and has led to incremental changes in existing policy and legislation. It has not, however, fostered ownership of and commitment to this agenda by domestic politicians and administrators.

Recommendations

Generating and sustaining political will is crucial to achieving gender equality in education, and it requires sustained commitment, leadership, and responsiveness on the part of decision makers. Political will and state capacity go hand in hand, and those countries in which political will has been joined with capacity to deliver have made the greatest progress towards gender equality in education. But without the capacity of a government to make and implement policy, the most well-intended political commitments will remain unrealised. Moreover, without on-going pressure from communities and civil-society organisations, gains in gender equality are unlikely to be sustained. Specific recommendations for governments, donors and NGOs include:

Governments:

- Ensure the implementation and enforcement of legal commitments to gender equality.

- Make gender equality a national priority within a broad and strong commitment to social inclusion.

- Create opportunities for women leaders within government, and ensure the sustainability of these positions.

- Play a stronger role in monitoring and regulating the activities of alternative providers.

Donors:

- Continue to be strong advocates for gender parity and to put girls' education on the agenda.

- Foster ownership of and commitment to this agenda by domestic politicians and administrators.

- Encourage and assist NGOs to create the kind of central leadership and grassroots support that can sustain effective campaigning.

NGOs:

- Maximise the kind of central leadership and grassroots support that can sustain effective campaigning and advocacy for gender equality over time.

- Promote women's leadership within civil society to demand sustained change.

- Work to gain the support of traditional and religious leaders in promoting girls' education at both national and local levels.

Notes

1 Political will and capacity development go hand in hand. The role of capacity development is discussed in Chapter 6.

2 L. Semu (2003) 'Malawi Country Study', background paper for the Global Campaign for Education.

3 K. Hyde, A. Ekatan, P. Kiage, and C. Basara (2001) 'The Impact of HIV/AIDS on Formal Schooling in Uganda', Brighton: Centre for International Education, University of Sussex.

4 See Chapter 6, which discusses the ways in which institutions, practices, and priorities within organisations may be 'gendered' in a way that is disadvantageous to women and girls.

5 Adapted from K. Hyde and S. Miske (2000) 'Girls' Education', background report for Dakar World Conference on Education for All, Paris: UNESCO.

6 E. Kane (2004) 'Girls' Education in Africa: What Do We Know About Strategies that Work?', Africa Region Human Development Working Paper Series, Washington DC: World Bank.

7 E. Kadzamira and P. Rose (2005) 'Non-State Provision of Basic Services: Education in Malawi', paper prepared for the Non-State Provision of Basic Services Programme, DFID.

6. Developing capacity to achieve gender equality in education

Failure to achieve gender equality in education is often blamed on 'weak capacity'. This chapter illustrates the ways in which individual, organisational, and institutional capacity all play important roles in producing positive results for girls and boys. It is essential to recognise that these different forms of capacity are related, in order to prevent the disappearance of policies and strategies produced with the aim of achieving gender equality in education.

Defining capacity

The capacity of a country to deliver on commitments to gender parity and equality in education is determined by individuals and the organisations in which they work, and also the bureaucratic systems in which they operate. Improving the capacity to deliver on gender equality in education targets often entails capacity development at all these levels.[1] This chapter focuses on transforming institutions and developing capacity of those working with education institutions, but it recognises that long-term capacity building for civil society, communities, and parents is also essential for taking forward gender equality.

Individual capacity

Individual capacity comprises the quality, skills, and commitment of each policy maker, administrator, and teacher. Teachers must be able to teach both girls and boys effectively to ensure that gender inequalities are not strengthened in the classroom.

Senior administrators should be able to carry out gender analysis, to identify approaches as a result of this analysis, to help put these approaches into practice, and to monitor progress.

Gender training can play a significant role in building the capacity of administrators and teachers. Effective training needs both to raise awareness of gender issues and also to build the ability to carry out gender analysis over a sustained period as a normal practice. Training should ensure that all staff have an understanding of the importance of gender issues, in relation to their work. However, effective gender-training programmes also need to create specialists in gender issues, who possess the necessary skills for gender analysis, implementation, and monitoring.

Teachers can contribute to the achievement of the third Millennium Development Goal (MDG) ('promote gender equality and empower women') by developing new skills and capacities. Through their direct actions they can challenge received ideas of how girl and boy pupils behave, raise awareness of gender issues, and protect children against abuse that is a result of their sex. They can also encourage girls to take subjects traditionally considered appropriate only for boys, such as mathematics. Teachers, however, often lack the training to campaign for gender equity in schools.

There is no template for effective gender training. However, its impact is likely to be greater when it is prioritised, and endorsed by senior-level administrators and politicians. It is also likely to be more effective when it is not treated as a one-off event, and is instead integrated into broader training and changes to the institutions' systems.

Organisational capacity

In order to enable teachers and educational administrators to work effectively, the organisations in which they work (for example, schools and ministries of education) must have the capacity to fulfil their mandates. They may be constrained by insufficient numbers of personnel and inadequate financial systems, poor management, ineffective systems and processes for decision making, and inadequate information gathering and analytical capacity.

Institutional transformation

The way in which an institution is organised to take into account the different needs of women and men is often an obstacle to implementing reforms aimed at achieving gender equality in education. This may manifest itself in both practical and physical arrangements. For example, work arrangements often do not take account of domestic roles, such as child care, which are often the responsibility of women. They may also reflect female or male characteristics in terms of management styles, organisational principles, and the delegation of authority.

Box 6.1 Some resources for gender training and analysis in education

These are some of the increasing number of good materials that are easily available for practitioners; they can be easily adapted by trainers to suit the local context and the learners:

Practising Gender Analysis in Education, Oxfam Skills and Practice Series, by Fiona Leach. This book draws on a number of well-known analytical frameworks from the gender and development literature and suggests modifications to suit educational settings, with case studies and examples. These frameworks can be used for analysing capacity constraints within the education sector.

A Toolkit for Promoting Gender Equality in Education, by the Gender in Education Network in Asia (GENIA). The toolkit provides a range of resources developed by the UNESCO Network for practitioners (especially 'gender focal points') to provide awareness of planning and strategy behind the development of a participatory gender workshop. It includes guidance and tools to create gender-responsive Education for All plans.

Resource Pack: Pedagogical Strategies for Gender Equality in Basic Education. Developed for a teachers' workshop in Kenya, it provides a brief and accessible introduction to gender approaches and skills to enhance gender-sensitive ways of working for teachers with practical activities and definitions.[2]

Creating the ability to achieve the gender MDG therefore often requires the transformation of deep-seated relations between women and men, and their practices within organisations. Without such changes, there is a danger that reforms aimed at achieving gender equality in education will become insignificant.

Box 6.2 Transforming gender relations within an NGO: experience of BRAC

The Bangladesh Rural Advancement Committee (BRAC) is heralded as an NGO committed to achieving goals of gender equality through its education programmes and other initiatives. Changes within the organisation that take into account the different needs of women and men have also received attention, especially efforts to recruit, retain, and improve the effectiveness of female development workers. This has been done through adapting the organisational culture to better enable the participation of women (for example through introducing flexibility into the working day, and providing support for child care), increasing the participation of women in decision making through recruitment and promotion policies, including special management-skills training, and supporting women's physical needs, for example by providing appropriate accommodation, transport, health care, and maternity leave.

These policies allow views of men's and women's roles in both private and public spheres to be questioned. The recognition of the need to challenge conventional male work patterns within a dominant organisational culture, and the need to be open to change, has helped to improve the participation of women in BRAC. Transformations of this kind can take time and sustained effort and need to be well-resourced.[3]

Quotas for women

Quotas, if implemented with appropriate support as part of a wider process for promoting and sustaining gender equality, can increase women's visibility and challenge male dominance within organisations. A successful quota programme includes measures to develop the women's capacity so that their *presence* translates into *influence*.[4] Without this dimension, quotas are only symbolic, with women continuing to play a relatively minor role, either because of the types of responsibility they are given, or because of their own lack of confidence, or because of other commitments which prevent them from carrying out their work effectively.

In local-government structures in India and Pakistan, one-third of seats are reserved for women. In village education committees in some states in India, the chair or vice chair of the committee is required to be a woman. While some have criticised these measures because, for example, they can result in female relatives of powerful men taking these positions, others have pointed to the ways in which women in local government have successfully raised local issues concerning land, water, health, and education and have spoken their own minds, independently of the political affiliations of male relatives.

In Ethiopia, quotas for ensuring that one third of the intake into teacher-training institutes are female, have helped to ensure an increase in the availability of female teachers, who can be an important influence on the education of girls. However, since women are accepted with lower qualification levels than men, their performance tends to continue to lag behind, which may badly affect their self-esteem. To address this, the Women's Affairs Office in the Ministry of Education has designed training programmes to give additional support to women in these colleges, at the same time as providing them with assertiveness training.[5]

Gender mainstreaming within organisations

Gender mainstreaming is a strategy to promote gender equality within an organisation.[6] Mainstreaming has received particular attention since the 1995 Beijing World Conference on Women.

Mainstreaming is about extending concern for gender equality and education from a few vocal people, often on the periphery of organisations, to the centre of the development agenda. This requires rethinking of institutional rules, priorities, and goals, and substantial redistribution of resources.[7]

Within education, gender mainstreaming is often associated with sector-wide approaches (SWAPs) and poverty reduction strategy papers (PRSPs). Many countries' SWAPs and PRSPs contain broad commitments and specific strategies towards achieving gender equality. These commitments, however, are often made without considering whether there is capacity to implement them.

Gender-mainstreaming strategies may be either diffuse or specific. On the one hand, gender equality can be made the responsibility of everyone in the organisation, with related concerns incorporated into all organisational structures and activities. There is, however, a danger that this diffuse approach will sideline gender issues, as other concerns are given higher priority. It can also reduce gender analysis to an insignificant function. On the other hand, specialist units may be set up within ministries of education to ensure that gender issues are visible and endorsed by all levels of the organisation.

In countries in both South Asia and sub-Saharan Africa, support for girls' education has often been the responsibility of separate 'gender focal points', either within the Ministry of Education or as a separate ministry or unit. Ideally, focal points act as *catalysts* of change, by working with individuals, departments, and ministries to raise gender awareness and ensure that gender parity and equality is incorporated into major policies, programmes, and procedures.

In practice, however, focal points have often been separated from usual planning activities within ministries of education, and they lack the resources and status to influence policy and programme priorities. In many cases, the roles and responsibilities of 'gender focal points' are inadequately defined and insufficiently resourced. The offices often rely on external funding, because resources are not available internally to support them. In addition, appointments to posts within these offices are often made at a low level, with limited opportunity for transfer or promotion.

Box 6.3 Gender initiatives in practice in Ethiopia and Guinea

Although Ethiopia is currently lagging behind in achieving universal primary education and gender equality, it has made considerable progress over the past decade as a result of a high-level commitment to establish Women's Affairs Officers at national, regional, and district levels. Through a nationally driven strategy of ensuring that gender is integrated into education planning, there is optimism that gender equality will be achieved. While this approach requires longer-term commitment, it should ensure greater sustainability than more gradual approaches to gender reforms.[8]

By comparison, in Guinea an Equity Committee was established in 1992, with the support of the then Minister of Education. This was successful in gaining the support of traditional and religious leaders and other public figures for the government's policy of encouraging girls' education. However, subsequently the committee has had no operating budget or strategic plan, as well as few personnel (most of the members work only part-time). As a result it has only been able to focus on random, short-term projects, with financing from NGOs and donor agencies.[9]

Whether one uses a targeted approach through 'gender focal units', or relies on merging responsibility for gender issues across organisations, one needs to consider the background and the timing. A more targeted approach is likely to be more effective in cases where organisational capacity is weak, and there is no evidence of a sustained political commitment to gender equality. If it is handled appropriately, and all stakeholders in the design and implementation process are involved, this strategy could support political commitment to a more coherent approach in the longer term. In practice, across ministries of education in developing countries, there is little evidence of successful integrated approaches to gender mainstreaming.

Recommendations

Developing capacity for gender equality involves implementing a range of strategies, comprising not only gender training of both male and female administrators and teachers to raise awareness and to provide necessary skills for gender analysis, but also initiatives to increase women's visibility within organisations, for example through using quotas. Developing capacity means focusing on gender concerns within organisations, and making gender issues an integral part of educational planning processes. The appropriate allocation of financial resources must be built in to these processes for them to succeed.

In many countries, governments are under pressure to implement a proliferation of policies while suffering severe financial constraints. Officials are often required to perform new roles, while carrying out existing ones more effectively. A priority for donors, therefore, should be to finance and strengthen individual and organisational development and capacity to achieve gender equality at the national level.

SWAPs and PRSPs provide a potentially valuable tool for capacity building. Evidence from the first phase of SWAPs in education in countries such as Uganda and Bangladesh indicates that although gender targets and strategies are included in these documents, budgets are not large enough to support them. The second phase of plans in these countries allocates more resources to capacity building and gender programming. The growing trend towards the preparation of budgets that take into account gender issues can also help to ensure that sufficient resources are committed and used to support gender equality in education.[10]

International agencies also need capacity for high-quality gender analysis, programming, and advocacy. Most agencies are making progress on developing the capacities of important individuals, but increasing organisational capacity and improving institutional incentives require more sustained effort.

Governments:

- Address the need to build capacity at individual, institutional, and organisational levels.

- Ensure that *all* staff have an understanding of the importance of gender issues in relation to their work, and that gender specialists possess the necessary skills.

- Integrate gender training and analysis through all programmes of teacher education, to help teachers to be effective change agents.

- Develop gender-sensitive budgets to ensure that adequate resources are committed to achieve the MDGs, and to monitor their use.

Donors:

- Finance individual and organisational development for gender equality at the national level.

- Ensure SWAPs and PRSPs include realistic budgets to implement gender-equality strategies.

- Ensure that donors themselves are improving their capacity to support high-quality gender analysis, programming, and advocacy.

NGOs:

- Ensure that NGOs themselves are improving their capacity to transform gender relations in their own work, and in the way they work with others.

- Support governments to build capacity for gender equality through working with planners in ministries of education.

- Monitor progress on capacity building for gender equality at the local level, and use this to influence government and donor policy at the national level.

- Support local organisations, schools, and communities to participate in gender-sensitive monitoring of education.

Notes

1 Capacity is intimately related to political will. The role of political will is discussed in Chapter 5.

2 UNESCO (2004) 'A Toolkit for Promoting Gender Equality in Education', Gender in Education Network in Asia, UNESCO, Bangkok; F. Leach (2003) *Practising Gender Analysis in Education*, Oxfam Skills and Practice series, Oxford: Oxfam GB; Beyond Access (2004) 'Resource Pack: Pedagogic Strategies for Gender Equality in Basic Education', Beyond Access Workshop, Nairobi, Kenya, http://www.ioe.ac.uk/efps/beyondaccess.

3 A. Goetz (1997) 'Getting institutions right for women', *Gender and Development* 5(1).

4 A-M. Goetz (2003) *No Shortcuts to Power: African Women in Politics ad Policymaking*. London: Zed Press.

5 P. Rose (2003) 'Out-of-School Children in Ethiopia', Report for DFID-Ethiopia.

6 For a definition of gender mainstreaming see Chapter 1.

7 N. Kabeer and R. Subrahmanian (1996) 'Institutions, Relations and Outcomes: Framework and Tools for Gender-Aware Planning', IDS Discussion Paper 357, Brighton: IDS.

8 P. Rose (2003), *op. cit.*

9 A. Marphathia (2000) 'USAID/WIDTECH Technical Assistance and Training Plan to the Ministry of Pre-University and Civic Education's Equity Committee,' Washington: WIDTECH.

10 For a discussion of gender budgeting, see Chapter 7.

7. Gender-responsive budgeting in education

In the mid 1980s, the Australian government embarked on the first initiative to analyse government budgets from a gender perspective. In 1995, South Africa and the Philippines became the second and third countries to attempt gender-responsive budget exercises. By 2003, there had been similar initiatives in more than 60 countries, spanning every continent. This chapter uses the gender-responsive budgeting approach to explain how governments and donors can promote gender equality in education through their decisions on financing.

What is gender-responsive budgeting?

Gender-responsive budgeting (GRB) initiatives are very diverse, but they all have in common one essential question: *What is the impact of the government budget, and the policies and programmes that it funds, on women and men, girls and boys?* GRB is thus an attempt to ensure that gender-related issues are considered and addressed in all government policies and programmes, and specifically in the budgets allocated to implement them.

By 2003, GRB initiatives had been undertaken in more than 60 countries, spanning all the continents.[1] They differ significantly from one another, for a range of reasons that include the political and social conditions prevailing in the different countries, and the nature of the actors undertaking the activities. The availability of the budget and other supporting information for public scrutiny and the nature of the budget format will also lead to different approaches.

Some GRB initiatives have been undertaken by governments, some by parliamentarians, and some by civil-society groupings. Where parliaments undertake the exercise, it is part of their role of overseeing a government's budget. Where civil society plays a role, it is usually linked to advocacy for reform. However, groups from government and civil society may work together, with overlapping aims.

GRB initiatives are known to have been undertaken in connection with education in the following countries: Kenya, Malawi, Mauritius, Mozambique, Namibia, Rwanda, South Africa, Tanzania, Uganda, Zimbabwe, Barbados, Bangladesh, Malaysia, Nepal, Pakistan, the Philippines, and Sri Lanka.

Box 7.1 Some examples of gender-responsive budget initiatives

In South Africa, the Women's Budget Initiative was the result of action by parliamentarians in the Joint Monitoring Committee on Improvement of the Quality of Life and Status of Women in the first post-apartheid national legislature in 1994. Research and analysis for the Initiative was carried out by two non-government organisations (NGOs). The parliamentarians had a high level of legitimacy and were well placed to take forward the findings of the GRB initiative.

In Tanzania, a gender-focused NGO first undertook a GRB research and advocacy exercise in 1997. The government, prompted by donors, subsequently embarked on its own GRB exercise. In 1999, the government contracted the NGO to provide advice and training on GRB.

In Rwanda in 2002, the Ministry of Gender and Women in Development, supported by the UK government's Department for International Development, worked together with the Ministry of Finance in leading the GRB.[2]

What can GRB tell us?

Most GRB initiatives involve a process of analysis of some sort, although the processes will be different in different contexts. Internal government initiatives require that civil servants analyse the budget in gender terms before they decide how to change it. In parliamentary initiatives and those taking place outside government, the budget is analysed to understand what it means in terms of gender equality.

The South Australian GRB used a simple framework which has since been adopted and adapted in many other countries. This framework distinguishes between three categories of expenditure, as follows:

- **Gender-targeted expenditures**, i.e. expenditure directed specifically at improving gender equality. In terms of education, one example would be special scholarships for girls.

- **Staff-related employment-equity expenditures**, i.e. expenditures that promote employment equity among public servants. In education, they might include expenditures on training for women teachers to help them to progress further in their careers.

- **General/mainstream expenditures**, analysed for their gendered impact; for example, expenditure on post-compulsory education, sectors which commonly have a high proportion of male students; and the provision of early childhood education, because it particularly benefits women and older girls by reducing their burden of child care.

This chapter uses these three categories to discuss how education budgets in different countries have tried to promote gender equality.

Gender-targeted expenditures

Gender-targeted expenditures are the most easily visible in a government's budget. GRB initiatives should, however, avoid focusing only on this first category, because it usually accounts for only a tiny fraction of public expenditure. There is a risk that disproportionate attention will be focused on these small expenditures, while other programmes and associated budgets continue to operate with little or no consideration of gender equality. It is nevertheless important to consider this category of expenditures, because it constitutes a form of 'affirmative action' – the visible extra push that can start dislodging long-standing inequalities.[3]

The school stipends paid to girls in Bangladesh are among the best-known of targeted gender expenditures within the education sector. A recent evaluation[4] of the stipends acknowledges that the enrolment of girls has improved significantly since they were introduced. Adolescent girls are now visible in large numbers, going to and from school in rural areas – in itself a fundamental change.

However, the study argues that the introduction of free tuition may play an equal (or even stronger) role in increased enrolment than stipends do. Because the two initiatives were introduced more or less simultaneously, it is difficult to distinguish their impacts. The stipends are expensive: in 1998/99 those at secondary level accounted for 14.5 per cent of the total budget for secondary education, and for 6 per cent of the total education budget. The Female Stipend Program, then, is one of many initiatives in Bangladesh, but it is credited with also having had a positive impact on the enroloment of girls in primary school.[5]

83

The stipends have prompted concerns about corruption. A household survey conducted by Transparency International Bangladesh in 2005 found that, in the case of girl students at the secondary level, 22 per cent of those entitled to receive the stipend had to pay the government an average of 45 Taka in order to enroll in the scheme. In addition, five per cent of primary-school students and 38 per cent of female secondary-school students stated that at the time of payment a portion of their stipend was deducted by the authority.[6] These concerns raise awareness of the need for greater transparency in the administration of the stipends.

There are also questions to be asked about the equity of some of the gender-targeted expenditures once one looks beyond gender to other dimensions such as social class. In Rwanda, for example, schools for girls from disadvantaged families were established by the Forum for African Women Educationalists (FAWE); but some observers alleged that places in these schools were allocated to girls from richer families. In Zambia, UNICEF's Programme for the Advancement of Girls in Education (PAGE) is perceived to have created schools which are high quality but unrepresentative of and isolated from mainstream schools. These examples demonstrate that allocating specific expenditure to girls' education does not necessarily or adequately address the issue of girls' disadvantage due to poverty.

Bursary schemes are a common form of targeted gender expenditure. These schemes are usually small and thus benefit a limited number of children. There is a danger that the 'mainstream' bursary and loan schemes aimed at all children pay no attention to gender balance, on the grounds that the girls' needs are met by the targeted schemes. A more promising approach in countries that operate significant 'mainstream' schemes might be to incorporate quotas or affirmative action of some other kind into the general allocations. In 2005 this approach was being considered in Rwanda.

Targeted expenditures have often been funded by donors rather than by government; but they must address the vital question of sustainability: what will happen when donor funding for such expenditures ends, and what indicators will be used to decide when the affirmative action is no longer needed?

Staff-related expenditures

Staff-related expenditures are important because a large proportion of most government budgets in education and other social sectors is spent on salaries and related costs. It is therefore necessary to analyse the total sum spent on salaries, and the proportions spent on the salaries of men and women.

Free education, while not a guarantee of gender equality in education, can bring significant benefits for girls. But free education costs a lot of money. Like any scheme to expand education provision, it requires that many more teachers are employed, and at good levels of pay if quality is to be maintained. This may leave little public money to pay for other items, such as textbooks. Some sources (including the World Bank) have suggested that one solution to this problem is to employ teachers who are less well qualified, at lower rates of pay. In many contexts such teachers are women. This solution is, however, clearly self-defeating. It is 'economic' in narrow terms; but it is not effective, because it will not provide children with a good education. In addition, low salaries will encourage teachers to engage in secondary occupations, or attend workshops rather than teach, in order to benefit from the attendance allowances, which results in neglect of their teaching duties.

A low-salary solution to budget problems usually disadvantages women disproportionately. This happens because the lowest salaries are usually found at the primary level, where women teachers predominate. Science and maths teachers often receive higher salaries in order to fill posts in shortage subjects, and these are areas in which fewer women teachers are found.

Box 7.2 Analysing the equity of education expenditure Tanzania

Research by the Tanzania Gender Networking Programme (TGNP) in the mid 1990s found that 94 per cent of government employees, many of whom were teachers, were earning less than 65,000 Tanzanian Shillings (US$105) a month. TGNP contrasted these low salaries with large expenses benefiting people at the top of the hierarchy. For example, 35.7 million Tanzanian Shillings were allocated by the Administration and Personnel Department for 'special expenses' for the Minister, Deputy Minister, and Principal Secretary. The special expenses included the purchase of furniture and household items for the officers concerned. TGNP pointed out that the money could have been used instead to provide for an additional 30 female students at university, or scholarships for 500 female students at secondary school, or primary education for at least 1600 students.[7]

General/mainstream expenditures

The introduction of universal and free primary education (UFPE)[8] into a country is probably the most dramatically obvious application of mainstream expenditure that is likely to contribute to gender equity.

Some people argue that UFPE is not the answer to gender disparities in education, because such disparities usually remain after fees are abolished. This argument is flawed. Firstly, if the level of enrolment significantly increases for both boys and girls after UFPE is introduced, as it invariably does, this represents progress for girls, even if the gender disparities remain the same. If, as often happens, the gender gap narrows, it represents even more of an advance. In Uganda, Universal Primary Education, introduced in 1997, increased the primary net intake rate from 33 per cent for boys and 31.7 per cent for girls in 1991–1995 to 93 per cent for boys and 90 per cent for girls in 1997. This is clear evidence of progress.

A significant increase in girls' enrolment was ensured in Uganda by the fact that the government provided free education for four children per family, on condition that at least two of these should be girls if there were girls in the family. But even without this ruling, UFPE is likely to promote girls' enrolment, in that previously, when fees were charged, families would often choose to educate sons rather than daughters. The reasoning being that boys are considered more likely to stay in the family and support it later in their lives, while most girls would marry into other families. Once the cost of schooling is removed (or at least reduced), this boy-friendly bias in incentives for the family becomes less compelling.

Focusing on mainstream expenditure rather than special gender-related expenditures does not inevitably mean a lack of targeting. There is a range of ways in which targeting can occur within mainstream expenditure, without making separate allocations. One such means of targeting involves redistributing funds across education levels.

In a small number of countries, women outnumber men at all educational levels, including tertiary. But in most low-income countries, very few women usually reach tertiary studies – yet spending per higher-education student may be vastly greater than that on the average primary student. This is inequitable in terms of social class, because many poor children do not complete primary schooling; and it is inequitable in terms of gender, given the small number of women who benefit from the high tertiary expenditures. Shifting money to reduce the inequality in spending between tertiary and primary or secondary education will usually favour girls. In 1995/96, the Tanzanian government was spending more than 100 times as much on a single tertiary student than on a primary-school pupil, and the cost of educating a university student was 17 times that of educating a secondary-school student.

Countries spend significant proportions of their education budgets on primary, secondary, and tertiary education. Generally the debate focuses on the relative proportions allocated to these three levels. What is often neglected is two other levels: adult education and literacy, and early childhood education and development (ECED). The provision of adult education and literacy for women contributes to broad social-development aspirations to achieve an end to poverty. ECED is important for women because it helps to lessen their burden of unpaid labour in terms of child care, and also frees them to engage in income-earning activities or social activities outside the home.

Box 7.3 Neglecting early childhood education at the expense of women

In the mid-1990s, South Africa was spending less than one per cent of its education budget on literacy, despite the fact that 23 per cent of South African women aged 20 years and above had never attended school. It was also spending less than one per cent of its education budget on ECED. This situation still prevails a decade later. Only 0.7 per cent of consolidated provincial education budgets for 2005/6 is devoted to ECED.[9]

The government did pilot the use of conditional grants (i.e. funds that could be spent only on ECED) to provinces, but the grants were under-spent and have now ceased. Upon this cessation, it was expected that provinces would contribute to ECED themselves, but this has not happened. Failures of both these strategies for funding arguably demonstrate a lack of leadership within the national Department for Education, which has failed to encourage provincial departments to spend some of their budget on ECED, and a lack of awareness of the issue of unpaid child-care work that is done mainly by women.[10]

A further form of targeting within mainstream expenditures focuses on gender or girls at the same time as attempting to address other forms of marginalisation. This is important because, while policies such as UFPE generally succeed in improving gender parity, problems in respect of enrolment often remain for poor people, for scheduled castes and tribes, and for migrant families and children living in remote rural areas. Initiatives introduced to address these sometimes ignore gender issues.

India's National Programme for Education of Girls at Elementary Level (NPEGEL) is an interesting attempt to address gender-based marginalisation and other aspects of disadvantage simultaneously, but without direct targeting.

Box 7.4 Addressing gender and marginalisation in India

The National Programme for Education of Girls at Elementary Level (NPEGEL) is a supplement to the Indian government's mainstream Sarva Shiksha Abhiyan (SSA) programme, introduced in 2001/2. SSA already supports some financial provisions for girls' education, including free textbooks. NPEGEL will focus on 'underprivileged/ disadvantaged girls' in classes I–VII in (a) areas where the level of rural female literacy is less than the national average and the gender gap is above the national average; (b) districts where scheduled castes/tribes constitute at least five per cent of the population, and the female literacy rate is below ten per cent; and (c) selected urban slums. 'Clusters' of schools which demonstrate good rates of enrolment for girls will receive extra money to allow them to provide things such as additional classrooms, clean drinking water, electrification, and toilets. NPEGEL will also provide money for child-care centres, to relieve older girls of this task.[11]

Other relatively low-cost strategies involve a 'reward' for institutions or local governments that perform well in respect of gender equality. The rewards could, for example, be built into resource-allocation formulas for local governments, as described above for NPEGEL.

There is also, however, a range of ways in which a focus on girls can be achieved within existing budgets. Examples include the following:

- Introducing a quota system for the selection of girls for the first year of secondary school or for university. (However, when quotas are introduced care must be taken to provide the necessary support to help girls succeed.)

- Requiring fewer 'points' from girls to qualify for admission to secondary or tertiary education. (This is done in respect of *men* in Kuwait.)

- Requiring that all community-built secondary day schools enrol and retain equal numbers of girls and boys.

- Requiring, as Uganda did, that where only a certain number of children per family can be provided with free education, at least half of these must be girls.

Recommendations

Governments:

- Support free education programmes, because they encourage improvements in girls' access to and retention in schools. The cost of implementing them effectively must, however, be acknowledged and planned for.

- Wherever possible, support gender equality in education through the mainstreaming of gender equality within other programmes. Adequate monitoring and evaluation mechanisms should be developed, to assess whether gender equality is being successfully mainstreamed.

- Determine before supporting donor-funded gender-specific initiatives that the expenditure will be sustainable if, and when, donor support ends; discuss and agree on the indicators and process for ending special programmes.

- In the interests of both reducing poverty and achieving gender equality, carefully consider the balance of expenditure between tertiary, secondary, and primary education; and consider a range of sources for funding the tertiary sector, including low-interest student loans, to be repaid over a period after graduation.

- Ensure that a concern to advance girls' education does not obscure the need for support in neglected areas such as women's literacy, early childhood development, and gender-balanced vocational education.

NGOs:

- Explore opportunities for work and/or campaigning with parliamentarians, based on a gender-budgeting exercise for education.

- Work with employees in the education sector to examine gender equity in terms of who is employed where, on what terms, and with what consequences.

- Support and encourage local organisations and schools to engage in their own GRB exercises.

- When planning campaigns for universal free education, examine the distribution of expenditure in the education sector as a whole, and ask who benefits.

- Link campaigns for universal and free primary education with wider initiatives to promote early childhood education and development, and adult education.

Notes

1   D. Budlender and G. Hewitt (eds.) (2002) *Gender Budgets Make More Cents*, London: Commonwealth Secretariat.

2   D. Budlender (2005) '*Girls' Education Paper – The Financing Issues*', background paper for Girls' Education: Towards a Better Future For All, London: DFID.

3   See also Chapter 8 for discussion of a twin-track approach focusing on (a) gender interventions and girls-only initiatives, and (b) improving access and quality for all children.

4   J. Raynor and R. A. Chowdhury (2004) 'A National Assessment of Girls' Secondary Stipend Programmes in Bangladesh', draft paper for DfID, Dhaka, Bangladesh.

5   J. Raynor (2005) 'Educating girls in Bangladesh: Watering a Neighbour's Tree?', in S. Aikman and E. Unterhalter (eds.) *Beyond Access: Transforming Policy and Practice for Gender Equality in Education*, Oxford: Oxfam GB.

6   Transparency International Bangladesh (2005) *Corruption in Bangladesh: A Household Survey*, available online at http://www.ti-bangladesh.org/documents/HouseholdSurvey200405-sum1.pdf

7   D. Budlender (2005), *op. cit.*

8   Different terms with different implications are adopted in different countries; for example, Kenya has introduced Free Primary Education (FPE), while Uganda and Tanzania have introduced Universal Primary Education (UPE).

9   R. A. Wildeman (2005) 'A Review of National and Provincial Education Budgets', occasional paper, Cape Town: Institute for Democracy in South Africa.

10   D. Budlender (2005), *op. cit.*

11   *Ibid.*

8. Girls' education in Africa

Sub-Saharan Africa has some huge problems to resolve if it is to achieve gender equality in education, and fulfil the Millennium Development Goals related to education and gender. Conversely, the region also has some of the most innovative and enterprising examples of initiatives that promote gender equality in education. This chapter focuses on sub-Saharan Africa and considers some of the most significant obstacles that African girls face in achieving the education that is their right. The chapter then reviews the most significant initiatives – those that are 'gender-neutral' and those that have a specific focus on gender equality – that have enabled African countries to overcome these obstacles.

How are African girls faring?

Neither boys nor girls are doing well in many sub-Saharan African countries, yet Africa has also some of the most innovative and dynamic examples of what works. For example, in the Forum for African Women's Education, (FAWE), Africa has a dynamic and active network for working for change in girls' education. But even where there are favourable enrolment trends, these can hide problems related to how girls progress through school and complete their education. In Africa, girls attend school for an average of only 2.82 years before they reach the age of 16. This is less than anywhere else in the world. Only 46 per cent of girls enrolling in school in sub-Saharan Africa complete primary school.[1]

At the current rate of progress, gender parity, that is equal numbers of boys and girls in primary education, in sub-Saharan Africa will not be reached until 2038. These figures do not tell us anything about gender equality more widely in schools or associated environments. The Beyond Access project developed the Gender Equality in Education Index (GEEI) in order to help measure wider progress in gender equality in education. The GEEI measures girls' attendance at primary school, their completion of five years of schooling, their enrolment in secondary school, and the levels of gender equality that girls will encounter as adults, in both health care and earnings.

Some countries in Africa, like Botswana, Namibia, and South Africa, currently have a relatively high GEEI score of over 60 (out of a possible score of 100). This is a considerable achievement, but the Beyond Access project estimates that a GEEI score of 95 would indicate that the Millennium Development Goals concerning universal primary education and gender equality were being met. Even the high-scoring countries in Africa will need a sustained effort over the next ten years if they are to reach 95. Another group of countries, including Uganda, Tanzania, and Ghana, have a GEEI score of less than 60, but have seen a steady rise in GEEI over the last ten years. This is associated with wide political mobilisation and the introduction of new approaches to learning and teaching. Some countries, including Kenya and Nigeria, which have the largest populations in Africa, saw a fall in their GEEI score between 1993 and 2003, and they are currently well below 60. They face a massive task to mobilise people and financial resources if they are to reach 95 by 2015.[2]

Africa is a diverse continent, comprising more than 50 countries, which includes a wide range of cultures, relatively wealthy countries, countries that are dependent on foreign aid, countries embroiled in civil wars, stable democracies, countries with relatively highly educated populations, and some with barely literate populations. When enrolment data are analysed by country, they reveal a wide range of different experiences, with Niger enrolling only 30 per cent of its girls in primary school (and 40 per cent of boys), compared with Uganda, which enrols well over 100 per cent of both girls and boys.[3] Girls in Central and West Africa tend to have the widest gap in enrolment compared with boys. In Guinea Bissau, for example, just over 60 per cent of girls and 100 per cent of boys enrol in primary school.[4] In more remote areas of Mali, government statistics indicate that girls' gross enrolment rates are as low as 29 per cent. If primary school enrolment figures for rural girls are so low, one can presume that the number of girls who complete primary and secondary school is extremely low.

Generalising about the status of girls' education in even a single country is often misleading. Variations within each individual country are substantial. Girls' educational development in different parts of Mozambique, for instance, varies widely for cultural, economic, and geographic reasons.

Religion, remoteness from urban centres, marriage practices, migration patterns, the burden of disease, seasonal labour requirements and cash flows, and other factors all contribute to the wide variety of reasons for girls' enrolment and retention differences within the same country.

There are more countries in conflict and 'low income countries under stress' in Africa than in any other region. These countries are characterised by a combination of weak policies, inadequate institutions, poor governance, and human-rights violations. Of the 17 sub-Saharan African countries in which enrolment rates declined in the 1990s, six experienced major armed conflict, in which girls were particularly vulnerable. Some estimates show that 50 per cent of out-of-school children live in conflict-affected environments. Countries with a low GEEI also have histories of conflict.

Box 8.1 Educating girls in conflict-affected countries

Services (including education) established in the context of emergencies or disasters are often provided with no regard to the sex of the recipients, and they often inadvertently exclude girls. Girls' particular vulnerabilities in terms of physical security, and their exposure to physical violence, are intensified in conflict or emergency situations.

Countries emerging from armed conflict are extremely challenging environments in which to work. However, post-conflict countries can provide unique opportunities. Rwanda is an example of a country in which development agencies were able to provide tangible support to the new government and its commitment to equity and inclusion.

Countries where a conflict is just ending, such as Sudan, are often faced with ruined or poorly maintained social and physical infrastructure. Discussions about refining policies to include girls are rarely practical when the vast majority of children are not receiving any formal schooling, but there are still important opportunities for promoting girls' education. Support for new schools, for example, can include design considerations that are beneficial to girls, such as separate latrines, school walls, and teacher accommodation appropriate for women. Curriculum development should entail including an understanding of gender issues in all subjects, including a more determined attempt to ensure that all teaching and learning materials take into account the needs of girls and boys.[5]

However, we can identify broad areas that need attention and support:

- The provision of education, such as schools, desks, books, and teaching and learning materials.

- The ability to determine the different needs of girls and boys, and a political commitment to girls' education.

- Administrative capacity, in ministries of education and in the wider civil service.

- Pay, conditions, and teacher deployment, as well as school management and regional supervision, data collection and analysis.

Across sub-Saharan Africa, with some countries excepted, donors dominate education funding, and tend to have more influence on education policy and practice than in other regions. There are high population-growth rates, with a higher percentage of the population under 15 years of age than in any other region. The burden of HIV, malaria, and TB in Africa is higher than in any other region, with substantial implications both for many countries' education systems, and also for school-age girls. Nevertheless, locally specific analysis of the differences experienced by girls and by boys, combined with sustained commitment and sufficient resources, produces the ideas and momentum to attract and keep girls in school.

Gender-equality initiatives have been hampered by policy makers underestimating the full range of economic costs to families and communities (especially non-fee and opportunity costs), as well as by ignoring relations and practices in the household and the community that are conditioned by the ways in which women and men interact. Developing 'islands of excellence' that do not take into account conditions elsewhere in the country (including financial constraints), and expecting single strategies to resolve complex problems, along with poor planning and imple-mentation, and the lack of a clear relationship between strategies and objectives, have also impeded attempts to ensure that girls and boys have equal opportunities.[6]

A dual approach to achieving girls' right to education

A dual approach involving two types of interventions is required in order to get girls in school and keep them there. First, getting the education system to perform for boys and girls is an essential step towards dramatic improvements in girls' opportunities and results, particularly at the primary level. But while this is a necessary step, by itself it is not enough. The second intervention, to get more girls in school and ensure that they complete their education, requires an approach that specifically targets girls.

Education systems accessible to boys and girls

Uganda's commitment to expanding access to education for everyone is illustrated by the increased primary intake after Universal Primary Education was introduced in 1997, rising to 93 per cent for boys and 90 per cent for girls.[7]

Select examples of other interventions that are 'gender-neutral',[8] but have been shown to be more beneficial for girls than for boys, include reducing the distance that pupils have to travel to school (for example, in Niger and Ghana); initial literacy being taught in the mother tongue (as has happened in Zambia); and introducing a sustainable feeding programme in schools (as in Kenya).

Gender analysis and focused interventions

However, 'gender-neutral' interventions are not sufficient to introduce gender equality into education. The second part of an approach to enrol and retain more girls in school is to use interventions that specifically target girls. High-quality analyses of the local and national situations for girls' education, linked to a focused intervention and budget allocation, are critical. These actions may be focused on girls themselves (for example, providing more places for girls in secondary schools), or on changing the 'gender relations' that affect girls' attendance and performance (for example, expectations by the girls' community of early marriage, or teaching styles that discourage girls' participation in the classroom). Even where equity is a prominent government concern – as in Rwanda – a common hazard is that gender equality is understood as a specialised girls' issue, not as a wider group of social relationships involving the distribution of authority between men and women.

No single approach will resolve everything. A variety of interventions and initiatives is needed to improve education for girls so that they achieve success in both primary and secondary school. All development partners require both creativity and discipline if they are to undertake a variety of interventions that focus on process, and they need to bring these interventions together within one plan for the education sector. A wide range of development and government workers, at different levels of the aid system, need to allocate the thinking, time, and money required to promote girls' education (from projects to poverty reduction strategy papers and budget support; from local government to ministry headquarters).

Long-term commitment to the process of improving girls' educational results is essential, as no single plan, intervention, or approach will resolve the complex issues underlying girls' lack of achievement. Commitment to the long-term goal of increasing girls' participation at all levels of the education system will require adjustments to policies, such as changing the school day to accommodate girls' chores in the short term, but also changes to attitudes, such as encouraging communities to rethink how much domestic work should be expected of school-age girls.

Costs

Reducing the costs of education has significant benefits for both girls and boys. Costs may take four forms:

- direct school fees (such as those abolished in Free Primary Education policies);

- indirect fees (such as Parent Teacher Association fees, teachers' levies, and construction fees);

- indirect costs (for example the prices of shoes and uniforms);

- opportunity costs.

However, education costs impact differently on girls, and changes in costs have disproportionate effects on girls' ability to access school. Abolition of direct fees often leads to an even greater increase in girls' enrolment than in boys'. Indirect costs, such as clothing, safety, and transport, are generally higher for girls, thus making it even harder for girls to access school than for boys.

The effects of opportunity costs on education are particularly powerful for girls. Opportunity costs relate to the 'services' lost by a family when their child attends school. Opportunity costs are particularly important to understand once the initial 'gateway obstacles' of direct and indirect fees are successfully overcome. The education of African girls incurs particularly high opportunity costs, because fuel and water collection, which are time-consuming and labour-intensive, are jobs usually allocated to school-age girls. Girls also provide care for younger siblings when parents work and community child care is not available. Girls often work as traders in local markets and engage in a range of money-making activities. Girls are particularly badly affected by the AIDS epidemic. Not only are they at greater risk of becoming infected with the HIV virus than are boys, but they are also much more likely to miss school in order to care for sick family members. Girls are also vulnerable to abuse on the way to school, as well as at school. Early marriage and bride price are important factors in the social life of many African communities. In much of Sudan, for example, the more education a girl has, the lower her bride price, which creates significant opportunity costs for parents.[9]

Addressing the underlying causes of these high opportunity costs of sending girls to school is complex, because they arise from deeply embedded relationships between females and males, which are specific to both the local community and also the wider economy. Interventions are needed that are not only diverse and far-reaching, but driven by community participation and inclusion.

Some examples of successful efforts include community schools, which provide education within a short school day that is organised around girls' domestic responsibilities, and which are combined with intensive lobbying of the community on the value of girls' education; the provision of early childhood education programmes, crèches, and other programmes that lift the burden of child care from school-age girls; the provision of water and fuel sources that do not require many hours of work for girls; plus other labour-saving or money-making initiatives. In the long term, it is necessary to change the conditions of the formal and informal labour markets, establish equal wages and conditions of work, and thus demonstrate that educated girls do have improved incomes and quality of life.

Improving the quality of education for girls in Africa

Improving girls' initial access to primary and secondary schooling – most obviously through reducing the costs of attending school – is an important step in the right direction. Many countries in Africa are still trying to work out how to make access to education affordable to all. The question of keeping girls in school through completion of primary and secondary school is another matter. School completion is very often closely related to school quality. The concept of quality encompasses a range of issues, including teaching methods and styles, infrastructure and school materials, school governance and community involvement, and curriculum.[10]

There are initiatives that have improved school quality and contributed to an increase in girls' completion rates in some countries (though without more systematic analysis one cannot generalise about their effectiveness, affordability, and relevance in different contexts).

These initiatives include:

- making girls' enrolment and progression rates a part of performance criteria (for both schools and their staff members);

- including gender awareness as an integral part of teacher training for both pre-service and in-service training and performance review;

- adopting education curricula and materials that recognise the needs of both girls and boys;

- providing separate latrines and other appropriate infrastructure;

- tackling gender-based violence and sexual harassment and reforming policy on the admissibility of pregnant girls;

- employing more female teachers in rural areas;

- allowing preferential access and allowing automatic progression for girls.

Recommendations

There is no one-size-fits-all answer to the problem of getting girls in school and keeping them there. Strategies will vary from country to country depending on whether the country has reached universal primary education, has a strong political commitment to women's equality, and/or has a relatively robust administrative capacity. At the most general level, however, a dual approach to promoting girls' education is needed in all countries which involves improving access and quality for all children as well as targeted programmes. Countries need also to improve the eduction system overall, including evidence-based planning, good financing systems and healthy budgets, minimal barriers to access, and attention to quality.

Governments:

- Ensure sufficient spending on primary and secondary education;

- Ensure free basic education at the point of delivery and removal of costs (direct/indirect fees, indirect/opportunity costs);

- Provide sufficient numbers of physically accessible schools;

- Ensure reasonable class sizes and teacher salaries;

- Support and promote targeted initiatives for girls from the poorest families and those from rural areas;

- Consider gender equality as an integral dimension of teaching and learning.

NGOs:

- Ensure that targeted initiatives are not 'islands of excellence' but are integrated into education plans;

- Provide good-quality monitoring and information gathering at the local level, for the development of good-quality education policies and practices that treat girls and boys equally;

- Campaign for a variety of approaches that focus on process and that are realistically priced;

- allocating the thinking, time, and money required to promote girls' education;

- Monitor government progress using specific tools, for example budgeting that reflects the different needs of girls and boys, or GEEI at district level.

Notes

1   E. Kane (2004) 'Girls' Education in Africa: What Do We Know about Strategies that Work?', Africa Region Human Development Working Paper Series, Washington DC: World Bank.

2   E. Unterhalter, E. Kioko-Echessa, R. Pattman, R. Rajagopalan, and N. Fatmatta (2005) 'Scaling up Girls' Education: Towards a Scorecard on Girls' Education in the Commonwealth', London: Beyond Access Project.

3   These rates are 'gross enrolment rates'. Gross enrolment rates can exceed 100 per cent as they include students over formal school-going age who are still attending primary school. Net enrolment rates include only students of formal school-going age and do not exceed 100 per cent.

4   UNESCO (2003) *Gender and Education for All – The Leap to Equality*, EFA Global Monitoring Report 2003/4, Paris: UNESCO.

5   See L. Yates (2003) 'Does Curriculum Matter?', paper presented at Beyond Access seminar, available at: http://www.ioe.ac.uk/schools/efps/GenderEducDev/Lyn%20Yates%20pre-summary.pdf; J. Kirk (2004) 'Teachers Creating Change: Working for Girls' Education and Gender Equity in South Sudan', Equals Newlsetter 8, September; D. Mazurana (2004) 'Reintegrating Girls from Fighting Forces in Africa', ID21 *Insights*, Issue 3.

6   E. Kane (2004), *op. cit.*

7   See Chapter 7.

8   'Gender-neutral' is the term most commonly used in the literature when referring to interventions that do not make explicit provisions for boys and girls. However, 'gender-blind' is a more accurate term for interventions that are not targeted.

9   In contrast, in much of Southern Africa, a more educated girl commands a higher bride price than a girl with less education.

10   See Chapter 1.

9. Girls' education in South Asia

Because of deep-rooted gender inequalities, and because of the large population of South Asia, the region has the highest number of out-of-school girls in the world. This chapter outlines some of the issues confronting practitioners, policy makers, and researchers in girls' education in South Asia, and explores what they can do to move towards high-quality and gender-equitable education for all.

South Asia at a glance

The South Asia region comprises ten per cent of the Asian continent, but its population accounts for about 40 per cent of Asian peoples. The South Asian Association for Regional Cooperation (SAARC), consists of Afghanistan,[1] Bangladesh, Bhutan, India, Nepal, the Maldives, Pakistan, and Sri Lanka. Although the SAARC countries have political and economic links, South Asia is a diverse region. Geographical and geological factors, as well as population and poverty, affect education systems in general, and the education of girls in particular. While there are gender issues in education in South Asia that have negative impacts on boys rather than girls – such as boys being more likely to be subjected to physical punishment, or being ineligible for benefits designed specifically to get girls into school – the focus of this chapter is on girls. This is because where there is poverty, or exclusion, or some other form of disadvantage, girls are far more likely to be adversely affected than boys. In terms of national development, a country cannot flourish if half of the population is left out of the development process.

How girls in South Asia are progressing

Although all members of the SAARC have signed the Convention on the Elimination of all forms of Discrimination Against Women, the Association has been slow to turn its attention to the gender inequalities so prevalent in all its member states. The autonomous Women's Advocacy Group was formed only at the eleventh summit, in Kathmandu in January 2002, with the task of 'getting gender on the agenda'. The group's first meeting was in Islamabad in June 2004, where various studies were commissioned, including one on female education and literacy. While that study is not yet available, the commitment to a sustained focus on gender issues was reiterated at the summit held in Dhaka in November 2005.[2] In the meantime, UNESCO estimates that nearly 24 million girls of primary-school age are not receiving education in South Asia.[3]

Indications of progress

There are no consistent links between overall human development, wealth, gender, or education in the SAARC countries. In each country, there are many interlinked factors that affect each indicator, and while we may be able to detect tendencies, we cannot say firmly that, for example, increased wealth means that a girl is more likely to be able to go to school. Bhutan, which spends more on education as a percentage of its total budget than any other SAARC country, has the lowest overall enrolment rate. However, overall in the region the average annual rate of increase in enrolment in primary education has been more than twice as high for girls as for boys during the period 1980 to 2001.

A measure of gender equality in education, developed by the Beyond Access project,[4] indicates that, while most countries in the region have shown an improvement over the past ten years, with Sri Lanka and the Maldives significantly ahead of the others, in Pakistan equality gaps have widened. The situation in Afghanistan will almost certainly have worsened too since 1990, but even in 2005 there are still no reliable data available. Bhutan is also likely to be a low scorer. Bangladesh stands out as the country that has made the greatest progress over the period 1990–2005, relative to other SAARC countries. It increased girls' secondary-school enrolment from 13 per cent to 56 per cent in ten years – a remarkable achievement for such a poor country – but a closer analysis of the figures behind the score shows that the progress is attributable to enrolment at primary and lower secondary levels, and that many other inequalities remain. Gender parity of enrolment does not tell us about parity or disparity in other areas of education.

Internationally agreed goals and targets

Some ambiguous features of the Millennium Development Goals (MDGs) and the Education For All (EFA) goals are apparent in South Asia. While Sri Lanka, Bangladesh, and surprisingly India have achieved the 2005 target of gender parity in primary education, Pakistan and Afghanistan are woefully lagging behind. Yet, while Bangladesh may have achieved parity of enrolment at primary and lower secondary levels, there is certainly not equality of achievement. The 2005 results for the Secondary School Certificate show that girls are less likely than boys to be entered for the final examination, and less likely to pass, and that these imbalances combine to make a 12 per cent gender gap in pass rates. There are similar disparities in terms of subject and school choice, and even bigger gaps at tertiary level. A focus on enrolment figures alone can lead to questionable conclusions. A quick look at the closing of the gender gap in enrolment in Bangladesh can lead to misleading assumptions that boys are now at a disadvantage. Overall, this is most definitely not the case, at least not in relation to girls.

India has recently introduced incentives similar to the Bangladesh secondary stipend programme, in which every family with a single girl child will be eligible for free education from Class 6. The motivation seems to be less of an EFA strategy than an attempt to control population (by keeping girls in school longer) and to redress the alarming population imbalance caused by son-preference.[5] However, as happened in Bangladesh, the secondary stipend will probably have a very positive indirect effect on primary enrolment for girls.

NGOs and community initiatives continue to play a role because, at present, agreed targets cannot be reached through the state system alone. Non-formal education schemes need to work with government to achieve EFA goals by targeting areas of high poverty, working children, children in geographically remote areas, and other hard-to-reach groups. In Bhutan, for example, with many children living in remote and inaccessible locations, communities are trying to provide equitable access by building their own schools, and providing hostel facilities for those girls and boys who live at a distance. An example is the Sengdhen Community Primary School, designed to serve disadvantaged children in seven villages in a remote part of the country that has been isolated for centuries. The most disadvantaged children also receive a scholarship of Nu (Ngultram) 1,500 (approximately $34) a year.[6]

Common issues and challenges

In this section, the main issues and challenges relating to girls' education in South Asia are divided into two categories: those that apply to both boys and girls but where the impact on girls might be more marked, and those that are issues for girls alone. The lists are not exhaustive.

Issues affecting girls and boys but with greater impact on girls

Quality of education

In 2000, at the E9 EFA forum in Recife, Brazil, the then Minister of Education for Bangladesh was able to report great progress in enrolment figures, but admitted: 'In our rush for numbers [after the 1990 agreements at Jomtien, Thailand], quality missed out'. This is true of many countries, not just Bangladesh, and across the region educational expansion often has been achieved at the expense of quality, with overcrowded classrooms, untrained or under-trained teachers brought in to deal with the increased numbers, and in some cases large proportions of the education budget being spent on financial incentives to get children into school. The struggle for universal access to education is fundamental to achieving gender equality, but complementary measures are also needed relating to the quality of educational provision, such as curriculum change, removal of prejudicial assumptions from textbooks, gender-sensitive training of teachers, and improvements to the learning environment.

The well known Bangladesh NGO, the Bangladesh Rural Advancement Committee (BRAC), addresses quality in its programmes in a variety of ways. Working closely with communities, BRAC offers a parallel and enhanced version of the primary curriculum, targeting poor families, illiterate parents, areas where child marriage is common, remote areas, and girls. The majority of BRAC teachers are local women. Beyond primary education, BRAC offers the Adolescent Development Programme (through *Kishori Kendro*), which was initially designed to ensure that adolescent girls did not lose their literacy skills on leaving school, but now is much more closely focused on life-skills and livelihood training. Empowerment is addressed in many ways, such as teaching girls about their bodies, or about laws that might affect their lives, but most impressively by handing the running of the centres over to the adolescent girls themselves.

Resources

Across the region, there are high levels of poverty, and inadequate resources. In the Maldives, there is no constitutionally guaranteed free education, and in Bhutan and Nepal fees are charged by primary schools, despite legally guaranteed free education. In other South Asian countries education is theoretically free, but parents are faced with unmanageable secondary financial demands. The call on limited financial resources can take on gender-based dimensions, with parents being more willing to invest scarce resources in sons than in daughters. For example, in many countries in the region, private tuition is needed to make up for the inadequacies of the education system, but such tuition is more often given to boys than to girls, thus lowering girls' chances of academic success.

Corruption

This issue is linked to resources, but is important enough to warrant separate attention. In the Framework of Action adopted by the World Education Forum meeting in Dakar, Senegal, in 2000, corruption in education was identified as a major drain on development. A recent study shows that the most common forms of corruption in education are parents being 'recommended' to buy materials written by the child's teacher; parents being 'advised' to pay for private tuition provided by the child's teacher; and parents being asked to contribute 'voluntary' donations for school infrastructure or extra-curricular activities.[7] As with resources in general, such demands are likely to have a more negative impact on girls than on boys.

Child labour

South Asia has the largest number of child labourers in the world. Children in 'day jobs' have problems attending school, and children who have to work before and/or after school are often too tired to get the maximum benefit from their schooling. Boys are more likely to be engaged in paid labour, but girls are increasingly being employed, because they can be paid even less than boys. In India, estimates for Andhra Pradesh alone indicate that there are 150,000 children aged 7–14 engaged in seasonal agricultural work, 90 per cent of whom are girls. Although they are formally enrolled in school, they are withdrawn for six to eight weeks at a time. Girls have the added burden of extra unpaid labour within the household, especially child-care responsibilities towards younger siblings, and a study in Bangladesh and

Nepal found that girls as young as ten often worked an average of ten hours a day. The more children have to work, the lower the likelihood of their getting a good education.

War and conflict

Three of the SAARC countries – Afghanistan, Nepal, and Sri Lanka – have been in long-term conflicts, and there have been recent periods of 'unrest' in other South Asian countries. The Beyond Access scorecards on gender equality and girls' education clearly demonstrate the negative effect of conflict on education in general, and on girls' education in particular. In Nepal, because of frequent kidnappings and raids, parents fear for their daughters' safety, and are withdrawing them from school. Thus the conflict threatens to undermine progress made in girls' enrolment. But in some countries, girls' education is not just a casualty in the conflict, but an actual target. Afghanistan is the most obvious example here, with reports in 2006 of a head teacher being decapitated, a teacher being shot for teaching girls, and parents being warned not to send their daughters to school.[8]

Natural disasters

The geological features of the region make it susceptible to natural disasters, such as the December 2004 tsunami that severely affected Sri Lanka, India, and the Maldives. The South Asia earthquake of October 2005 had devastating effects in Pakistan and India. Bangladesh is prone to regular and severe flooding. There are gender dimensions to such disasters. One is that women are more likely to lose their lives. For example, women's clothing makes them more likely to drown and they are less likely to have learned to swim or climb trees.

Other issues

There is not space here to cover all the gender-based dimensions of educational issues, but there are other challenges present to a greater or lesser extent in South Asia. Large cities in South Asia have many street children, most of whom have no access to education; the girls among them are even more vulnerable than the boys. HIV and AIDS is a growing concern, most notably in India, where 38 per cent of those affected are women; most formal education systems have yet to educate young people about the risks or prevention strategies, and girls are not taught that they have the right, for example, to insist that a husband use a condom.

Box 9.1 Emergency education response in Sri Lanka

After the tsunami hit Sri Lanka, an Emergency Education Desk was set up at the Centre for National Operations, and a Task Force was established to support the return of children to school by the end of January 2005. UNICEF provided major support, not only for the repairing and cleaning of damaged school buildings, but also for rebuilding child-friendly facilities which prioritised girls' needs, based on the following criteria:

- Children of primary-school age should have a school within walking distance.

- Learning spaces should include room for extra-curricular activities, project-based learning spaces, and individual learning spaces. Internal and external learning areas should be linked by verandas or decking.

- Communities (including children) should be involved in the locating, planning, and management of schools.

- Teachers should be supported to build links with the community and community-development initiatives. Teachers should receive training in providing psycho-social support for children and their families, and receive support themselves to cope with the trauma that they have undergone.[9]

Gender-specific issues

There are challenges that are linked simply to the biological fact of being female, with all the socially constructed gender values that surround that fact.

Missing girls and women

There are 50 million fewer women in South Asia today than there should be. Girl babies are killed before birth through sex-selective abortions, or they die prematurely through violence and neglect. According to the 2001 census, India has only 927 women per thousand men. States such as the Punjab, Haryana, Delhi, and Gujarat have between 79.3 and 87.8 girls for every 100 boys.[10] In theory, sex-selective abortion is illegal; in practice, it is widespread. If India succeeds in providing education for all, it will be impossible to achieve parity of enrolment in the near future because of these artificial disparities in the demographic profile. However, achieving quality education for all will in itself be a strong move towards eliminating the societal prejudices against women.

Marriage

Despite laws against the practice, child marriage is common throughout South Asia, and it effectively puts a stop to the educational progress of many girls. In Nepal, an estimated 40 per cent of girls are married by the time they reach the age of 15, having a husband being seen as more important than being educated. The giving or taking of dowry, also illegal, is common in South Asia, and, in general, lower dowry demands are made for younger brides, which adds to the temptation for parents to marry off their daughters while they are still young.

Bodily integrity

The issue of bodily integrity or sexual harassment becomes more urgent and oppressive the older a girl gets. In South Asia, sexual harassment is often referred to by the innocuous-sounding term 'Eve teasing', and it is widely reported in Bangladesh, India, Nepal, Pakistan, and Sri Lanka. A girl runs the risk of being harassed, assaulted, abducted, or even murdered on the way to or from school, and she is by no means free from risk within the school. For this reason, many girls are withdrawn from school when they reach puberty. Girls who live at some distance from the school are particularly vulnerable; the further they have to travel to school, the more remote the area, the greater the potential risk. Some parents compromise by sending their daughters to a nearby school, even if it is known to be of poor quality, or it does not offer the full range of subjects. The girls' brothers are allowed to go farther afield to find a better-quality education. In Madya Pradesh, India, the Education Guarantee Scheme has initiated the practice of para-teachers or helpers collecting girl children from their homes and dropping them off each day at school to ensure enrolment and security. Schools are constructed within a 1km radius from homesteads on demand and the emphasis is on enrolment of all children.

Innovative approaches to ensuring girls have greater and safer access to schools are extremely important, as are increasing the conditions for girls and boys to participate equally in learning. This means that gender equality needs to be a central part of the development of the school curriculum and ways of teaching (see Chapter 2).

Box 9.2 Learning about menstruation

While girls and teachers in India are aware of the taboos and sanctions pertaining to menstruation, which is seen as a polluting factor, they have little knowledge of the menstruation process itself. The Vacha Women's Resource Centre, in Mumbai, developed a teaching module for girls in western India based on a body chart made of cloth, layered with body parts attached with Velcro, which could be pulled apart and stuck back together. With these aids, and through discussions of girls' physical and social experiences, girls learned to distinguish socio-religious ideas about menstruation from biological processes. The girls raised many questions and shared the knowledge with their mothers.

Helping girls and women to change their perceptions of their bodies as being polluting agents will require multi-faceted strategies and long-term commitment, as these beliefs are supported by men, family members, caste, and religious systems.[11]

Nutrition

In many parts of South Asia, women and girls are expected to eat least and to eat last. That is, they get what is left over after the men and boys in the household have finished eating. This often results in a very poorly balanced diet, with little in the way of protein or vitamins. Malnutrition of course affects attentiveness and performance in school. In addition, many children leave school without learning enough about nutrition, and so traditions such as not eating 'rich' food during menstruation prevail, contributing to widespread anaemia. In India, it was found that girls living in villages where schools offer a free meal are 30 per cent more likely to complete primary education than other girls. To combat very high rates of malnutrition, the Indian government has now initiated a programme of universal midday school meals.

Teachers

It is generally assumed that women teachers provide good role models for girls in school; they allay parents' fears of security issues within the school, and their presence shows that the teaching profession is a suitable aspiration for girls currently in school. For some, the proportion of women teachers in the system is an indicator of progress, and there are fewer women teachers in countries with high gender disparities. In India, almost all single-teacher schools (about 20 per cent of all schools) are staffed by men, and over 70 per cent of two-teacher schools have no women teachers. However, a feminisation of the teaching profession – as can be seen in Sri Lanka and the Maldives, at least at primary level – may reinforce the impression of women as nurturers and carers.

Improving the quality of education for girls in Asia

This section provides some positive recommendations for the improvement of girls' education in South Asia, although there are many other examples. It should be stressed that while each example can have positive impact, all interventions are much more effective within a unified approach to gender and education. Concentrating on enrolment alone will not achieve the MDG target of a complete primary education for all by 2015. Clearly there is no one approach that suits all contexts, but at the very least there is a need for strategies which improve the overall access to and quality of the system for all children, and also a need for programmes that specifically target girls. What is needed, therefore, are multiple interventions developed and conceived within the framework of an overall education-sector plan, with clear linkages between all levels and types of education.

Recommendations

Governments:

- Develop coherent policy frameworks based on strong political commitment to gender equality and the mainstreaming of gender issues at all levels (see also Chapters 5 and 6).

- Ensure that all educational data is gender-disaggregated, so that inequities can be quantified and appropriate strategies devised to minimise imbalances and to target qualitative change.

- Implement legislation to make education free and compulsory and abolish fees and user charges for primary education.

- Introduce national programmes of extra support, such as cash transfers, stipends conditional on school attendance, free school meals, and scholarships.

- Ensure that such incentives are part of a comprehensive package for improving the quality and gender equality of education through the training of teachers, and the reform of the curriculum to provide meaningful and positive learning, ensuring that there are adequate resources in schools to meet increased enrolment.

Civil society and NGOs:

- Keep gender on the agenda of government at all levels through campaigning for strong political commitment to gender equality.

- Establish strong partnerships with government to support gender-sensitive programmes and policies in education.

- Document good innovative practices that improve gender equality in education for dissemination and advocacy, and document and learn from what does not work so well.

- Maintain attention on the gender dimensions of national and international goals and targets.

- Lobby for flexibility of educational provision to meet the special needs of girls.

Schools:

- Incorporate attention to gender issues in all teacher-education programmes.

- Focus on improving educational outcomes for girls – provide what is needed to enable them to stay in school, to learn what will be meaningful and empowering, to prepare them for paid employment, and for education to be seen as a suitable alternative to dowry.

- Remember that 'gender' is not just about girls and women, and ensure that boys in school today become the gender-sensitive husbands and fathers of tomorrow.

- Examine and remove gender stereotyping from school materials.

- Confront sexual harassment around and within places of education. (See also Chapter 2.)

Communities and parents:

- Be involved in any plans for education provision. There should be extensive consultation on what are seen to be the prevailing needs, and what are considered acceptable solutions. All consultations should include women and girls.

- Ensure that all community members are aware of the relevant laws, such as free or compulsory education, the age at which girls can be legally married, or the banning of dowry. Mobilise community members to support the enforcement of such laws.

Notes

1   At the summit held in Dhaka in November 2005, Afghanistan was admitted into the SAARC, with formal induction to take place at the next summit, hosted by India in 2007.

2   Source: http://www.saarc-sec.org/main.php?t=2.8.1.

3   UNESCO (2005) *Global Monitoring Report 2006: Literacy for Life*, Paris: UNESCO.

4   For details of the measure see E. Unterhalter, R. Rajagopalan, and C. Challender (2004) *A scorecard on girls' education in Asia, 1990–2000*. Bangkok: UNESCO, available at: http://k1.ioe.ac.uk/schools/efps/GenderEducDev/Asia%20Scorecard%20final.pdf.

5   J. Raynor (2005) 'Banglades: parity or equality?', *Equals* 15, p 3.

6   T. S. Powdyel (2006) *Schoolwise in Sengdhen*, on Kuensalonline. http://www.kuenselonline.com/modules.php?name=News&file=article&sid=6373.

7   See B. Meier and M. Griffin (2005) *Stealing the future: corruption in the classroom*, Berlin: Transparency International.

8   See D. Walsh (2006) 'Headteacher decapitated by Taliban', The *Guardian*; and N. Swainson (2005) 'Attaining Gender Equality in Primary and Secondary Schooling in Asia: progress to date and future priorities', a background paper for *Girls' Education: Towards a Better Future for All*, London: DFID.

9   Adapted from an article by Chloe Challender in *Equals* Issue 10, available at: http://www.ioe.ac.uk/efps/beyondaccess.

10 Oxfam International (2004) 'Towards Ending Violence Against Women in South Asia', Oxfam Briefing Paper 66, Oxford: Oxfam GB.

11 Adapted from an article by Sonal Shukla in *Equals* Issue 15.

Conclusion

The chapters in this book have raised a range of important issues for achieving gender equality and education for all. They have also provided some examples of innovative ways of addressing some of the issues and discussed some of the challenges in changing not only educational policies and practices, but also transforming structures that shape girls' and women's lives. The chapters argue for an education that promotes social change and contributes to building a just and democratic society; a society where education is a right and where girls and boys, men and women can exercise this right alongside their right to freedom from violence and discrimination and their right to life and livelihoods. This entails an expanded notion of gender equality in education that encompasses concern with empowerment and action, not just with equal numbers of girls and boys attending and completing school.

Transforming policy and practice for gender equality in education requires action by a range of different individuals working to put into practice particular ideas in different contexts and different types of organisation and institution. It requires understanding, capacity, political support, and adequate finances and management. It requires connections between different types of initiatives, because piecemeal, small interventions cannot adequately meet the challenges this book has outlined. As the chapters have shown there is already a lot known about what good quality gender-equitable education looks like and what happens when people put it into practice. Thus the way forward is reasonably well mapped out.

The chapters suggested actions and the different actors who need to be involved. This conclusion considers how these actions bear on the five challenges outlined in the introduction:

- Partnerships between practitioners, policy makers, and researchers
- Multiple interventions and actions
- Advocacy for policy and practice change

• Government commitment to and responsibility for basic education

• Adequate and sustainable financing.

The elusiveness of the goal for gender equality in education means that there is a need for a multiplicity of approaches and ways of working. The MDGs focus on the narrow dimension of gender parity and there is scant attention given to how gender equality relates to quality education or to the expanded notions of gender equality found in the Dakar Framework and the Beijing Platform for Action. A most pressing challenge is to build constructive partnerships between practitioners, policy makers, and researchers. Connections need to be made between the work of organisations working on women's empowerment and rights to gender equality, and those working on education quality. This entails building capacity, and promoting communication and co-ordination.

Then there are the groups that are not high on the MDG agenda; an agenda dominated by primary schooling and formal education. More consideration needs to be given to strategies for enrolling and supporting children in secondary school, addressing the gaps in adult education, paying attention to gender equality in education in societies experiencing or emerging from conflict, and assessing the effects of climate change and the HIV epidemic on gender and education aspirations.

Governments must lead the way on gender equality in education. While some governments have good policy, many lack the capacity to institutionalise gender equality and promote good practice. Moreover, they lack mechanisms for consultation with civil society, and consider gender-equality issues as second-order obligations, jostling for attention with addressing poverty, epidemics, or security.

There is the need for adequate funding to get every child into school and ensure that they receive a good quality education. But there is also a need to ensure that decisions on spending are underpinned by a serious commitment to gender equality. The future does not look assured on either of these issues. Gender audits need to be carried out to understand how money is being spent, to understand the funding gaps, and to scrutinise how extra financing for education is contributing – or not – to gender equality.

The recommendations below have emerged from the collaborative discussions carried out in connection with the Beyond Access project in the run up to 2005, the date set for achieving the first MDG target – gender parity. They are not a blueprint for the next ten years, but they do present a useful guide for working to ensure EFA is achieved in the fullest possible terms for every child. The recommendations look at three key dimensions of working for gender equality in education:

- planning, financing, and organisational development
- implementing gender equality within schools
- neglected groups.

Planning, financing, and organisational development

What can governments do?

The chapters in this collection highlight why it is important for governments to develop coherent policy frameworks based on strong political commitment to gender equality and the mainstreaming of gender issues at all levels. They make clear that significant achievements result when governments make gender equality a national priority within a broad and strong commitment to social inclusion. When governments are able to develop and implement indicators for quality and equality in education, they have accurate information on which to plan, allocate resources, and consult. They thus need to ensure that all educational data is gender-disaggregated, so that inequities can be quantified and appropriate strategies devised to minimise imbalances and to work towards qualitative change. Without these indicators the most needy may continue to be overlooked and experience discrimination.

While there is no guarantee that women leaders will necessarily advocate for gender equality, there are many instances that suggest women in leadership positions at every level of government help support and sustain initiatives for gender equality in education and help change the pre-conceptions on which much continued gender inequality rests. Many governments have legal commitments to gender equality enshrined in constitutions or key pieces of education legislation. But ensuring their implementation is a challenge. If strong legal measures to outlaw sexual violence and harassment in school (with clear procedures for dealing with abuse) are communicated widely, this can help create the conditions in which gender-equitable initiatives will flourish. The activities of alternative providers need careful monitoring and regulating.

Legislation to make education free and compulsory, and the abolition of fees and user charges encourage improvements in girls' access to and retention in schools. The cost of implementing these changes effectively must, however, be acknowledged and planned for. Donor-funded gender-specific initiatives may be an important adjunct to plans for gender-equitable education financed from local taxes, but expenditure planned through aid must be assessed in terms of what will be sustainable if, and when, donor support ends.

In the interests of both reducing poverty and achieving gender equality, governments need to consider the balance of expenditure between tertiary, secondary, and primary education. A policy push on increasing girls' access to primary school should not obscure the need to plan for support in neglected areas such as women's literacy, early childhood development, and gender-balanced vocational education. National programmes of targeted support, such as cash transfers, stipends conditional on school attendance, free school meals, and scholarships need to be explored. Such incentives should be part of a comprehensive package for improving the quality and gender equality of education through the training of teachers, and the reform of the curriculum to provide meaningful and positive learning, ensuring that there are adequate resources in schools to meet increased enrolment.

Governments need to pay careful attention to capacity building at individual, institutional, and organisational levels. This means governments which are serious about putting into practice the vision of the MDGs, EFA, and the Beijing Platform for Action need to ensure that *all* staff have an understanding of the importance of gender issues in relation to their work and understand the connections between education and other social sectors. A key step is to integrate gender training and analysis through all programmes of teacher education, to help teachers to be effective change agents. A second crucial move is to assess the planning and budgeting processes, and ensure that officials at all levels have the capacity to implement them in ways that take gender equity seriously.

These actions do not imply radically new action for governments; rather, they take gender seriously as a feature of the work they are already committed to. However, the challenges outlined above suggest that while mainstreaming gender in their existing work, governments should also be paying attention to a number of specific actions. These include: consulting with women and gender groups; considering frameworks and opportunities for exploring accountability with civil society; scrutinising expenditure in relation to its gendered effects; and considering whether the needs of the most marginalised are being addressed, particularly under changing conditions linked to climate, war, or increasing inequalities within a particular society.

What can donors do?

The large amounts of development assistance now earmarked for education, give donors an important opportunity to be strong advocates for gender equality and put girls' education on the agenda. They can help domestic politicians and administrators own and commit to this agenda by encouraging scrutiny of gender issues in all policy development, planning, and implementation, including sector-wide approaches (SWAps) and poverty reduction strategy papers (PRSPs). The challenges we have identified require donors also to look at the problems of fragmented networks and the lack of global and national leadership on gender equality and education issues. Donors can work with governments to assess particular needs in relation to gender equality in education and ensure good monitoring of how money is spent in relation to gender equality.

Donors have important opportunities to encourage and assist NGOs to advocate for gender equality. Their support in financing individual and organisational development for gender equality at the national level can help to build capacity that is so urgently needed. This means that donors themselves need to look to their own practice with regard to gender equality and improve their capacity to support high-quality gender analysis, programming, and advocacy.

What can NGOs and community-based organisations do?

NGOs and community-based organisations are important for identifying issues that may be beyond the view of government; ensuring accountability with regard to government actions; and promoting citizenship. Thus NGOs and community-based organisations need to ensure that they themselves, like governments, are improving their capacity to transform gender relations in their own work, and in the way they work with others. Building capacity for strategic planning around gender issues is an important form of organisational development. Key roles for NGOs and community-based organisations are to support governments to build capacity for gender equality through working with planners in ministries of education at all levels of government; to campaign for strong political commitment to gender equality; and to maintain attention on the gender dimensions of national and international goals and targets. Drawing on successful work from a range of contexts, some concrete steps include:

- Explore opportunities for work and/or campaigning with parliamentarians, based on a gender-budgeting exercise for education.

- Work with employees in the education sector to examine gender equity in terms of who is employed where, on what terms, and with what consequences.

- Support and encourage local organisations and schools to engage in their own gender-responsive budget exercises.

- Document good innovative practices that improve gender equality in education, for purposes of dissemination and advocacy, and document and learn from what does not work so well.

- Encourage community participation in schooling governance, involving women and men.

- Monitor progress on capacity building for gender equality at the local level, and use this to influence government and donor policy at the national level.

- Provide good-quality information gathering at the local level and support local organisations, schools, and communities to participate in gender-sensitive monitoring.

Some important dimensions that support these successes include building women's leadership within civil society and ensuring that targeted initiatives are not 'islands of excellence' but are integrated into education plans. In some societies, working to gain the support of traditional and religious leaders in promoting girls' education at both national and local levels can be a very significant first step.

Implementing gender equality within schools

It is not only gender-sensitive strategies in organisation and finance that will help develop and sustain gender equality in education. Schools and the processes of learning and teaching they promote are crucial to realising the outcomes of good planning. The challenges of fragmented global campaigning, lack of gender mainstreaming in government, inappropriate use of finances, and neglect of the most marginalised children will mark the learning experiences of girls and boys. It is particularly important that the everyday work of schools and teachers is alert to gender equality.

Governments and non-state providers of schooling should ensure that curriculum development involves consultation at all levels of society about gender equality, and that providers understand what their decisions mean for women and girls, especially those who may be marginalised because of language or social practice. Training in gender equality needs to be included in the teacher-education programmes, both in pre-service training and in-service college-based or school-based training. The capacity and role of the inspectorate and gender units to support gender equality in the classroom need to be enhanced.

Head teachers and teachers should develop school-level policies that ensure gender-equitable approaches to teaching and learning. This means that they need to confront sexual harassment around and within schools or education centres. They should be trained and empowered to analyse and challenge gender stereotyping and gender bias in curriculum materials, in language use, and in relations in the school and with the community. Support needs to be provided to help them understand their own culture, values, and aspirations with regard to gender – as well as those of their students and the surrounding community. There are many pressures on teachers, who need supportive networks that encourage change. Concern with 'gender' is not just about girls and women, but about relations of power and ideas about the future. Boys in school need to be encouraged to understand these relations too and to become the gender-sensitive husbands and fathers of tomorrow.

Parents and community members should take an active interest in their children's learning and ensure that the school learning environment is healthy and safe. In many countries they can play an active part in the planning and management of education resources so that they can ensure they benefit girls and boys equitably. It is important that parents and community members are aware of relevant legislation (such as a law enshrining education as free and compulsory, and the legal age of marriage for girls) and take an active part in ensuring the enforcement of such laws.

Neglected groups

Basic education and literacy for adults is a sorely neglected area of education. It has no MDG and often has no government policy, plan, or budget. Departments of Adult Basic Education are consistently starved of resources and status within hierarchies of ministry departments, and civil-society work in this area is often fragmentary. The continuing high level of women's illiteracy is one shocking result of this. Governments need to prioritise adult basic education and gender equality by developing a framework for adult basic education and literacy that is part of an integrated education policy. This integrated policy needs to link the concerns of women's groups with concern for gender equality across different sectors.

Prioritising financial and human resources and capacity at local levels of government for quality adult basic education and literacy that transforms gender relations is a key area for future work. Civil-society actors need to raise the profile of adult basic education and literacy and increase government commitment by lobbying for investment in adult basic education as a necessity for achieving all the MDGs, the Dakar Framework and the Beijing Platform for Action. Women's movements and organisations campaigning on HIV and AIDS and aspects of poverty are key to supporting civil-society organisations working on adult education.

Excluded and marginalised groups are most often those with least access to schooling. Even those groups that can participate, often receive the poorest quality of education. Government agencies need an analysis of the obstacles and inequalities faced by girls and women, inside and outside of the school in the most marginalised and exploited communities. They should ensure the availability of national-level cultural, economic, and social data on nomads, pastoralists, and other marginalised groups. This data should be disaggregated by sex and by region/province/district to inform education policy making. Government agencies should provide specific training for teachers to address linguistic and cultural differences and gender inequality, and concurrently promote the training of local teachers. The planning of policy frameworks and implementation strategies should involve the participation of marginalised groups and peoples, including women and girls, and their organisations, so as to take account of their rights of citizenship. Successful, innovative approaches to education with marginal groups, such as nomads and pastoralists, need to be examined with a view to positive lessons for their incorporation into decision-making processes.

Non-government agencies should raise the profile of excluded and exploited communities' education and specific needs. They have an important role to play in lobbying governments and donor agencies for adequate and sustainable financing, and for relevant and culture-sensitive and gender-sensitive education policies and practices.

The strategies we have outlined here in the recommendations are both wide-ranging and aspirational but they include some very practical steps. Different organisations, institutions, and individuals work in different ways and in different contexts. Some work with far-reaching and long-term perspectives and others with short-term actions. We are not advocating one approach or one particular place to start or finish, as this will be specific to particular settings. But the chapters in this book reveal both the broad spectrum of work that has already been started and the large number of tasks that still need to be accomplished. We are already half way toward 2015 and the dates set for achieving the MDGs and EFA. The MDGs are not distant hopes; they are very concrete goals and targets which we can all help to achieve.

Index